SUCCESSFUL GARDENING

CREATIVE GARDEN DESIGN

Staff for Successful Gardening (U.S.A.)
Editor: Carolyn T. Chubet

Contributors
Editor: Thomas Christopher
Art Editor: Joan Gramatte
Editorial Assistant: Troy Dreier
Consulting Editor: Lizzie Boyd (U.K.)
Consultant: Dora Galitzki
Copy Editor: Sue Heinemann
Art Assistant: Antonio Mora

READER'S DIGEST GENERAL BOOKS
Editor in Chief: John A. Pope, Jr.
General Books Editor, U.S.: Susan Wernert Lewis
Affinity Directors: Will Bradbury, Jim Dwyer, Kaari Ward
Art Director: Evelyn Bauer
Editorial Director: Jane Polley
Research Director: Laurel A. Gilbride
Group Art Editors: Robert M. Grant, Joel Musler
Copy Chief: Edward W. Atkinson
Picture Editor: Marion Bodine
Head Librarian: Jo Manning

Library of Congress Cataloging in Publication Data

Creative garden design.
      p.   cm. — (Successful gardening)
Includes index.
ISBN 0-89577-693-6
1. Gardens — Design.   2. Landscape gardening.   3. Gardens — Design
— Pictorial works.   4. Landscape gardening — Pictorial works.
I. Reader's Digest Association.   II. Series.
SB473.C736   1995
712.6'—dc20   94-39325

Opposite: Good garden design marries house with garden.
The whitewashed walls of a thatched cottage are tailor-made
for climbing wisteria, ivies, clematis, and roses.

Overleaf: A tiny town garden becomes a secret enclosure
of greenery ornamented with statuary, pots of lilies, and
ancient flagstones.

Pages 6-7: A suburban garden has lost its square shape
through a design of curved lines, raised planting areas,
and scree beds.

THE READER'S DIGEST ASSOCIATION, INC.
Pleasantville, New York / Montreal

SUCCESSFUL GARDENING

CREATIVE
GARDEN DESIGN

CONTENTS

Garden planning

Designs for small gardens

Designs for large gardens

Design for a purpose

Theme gardens

Curving lawn The rectangular shape of a suburban garden is softened by a lawn designed with gentle curves.

Garden planning

Few gardens meet with their owners' complete approval, for we all have different ideas about what constitutes a perfect landscape. Absolute perfection is not the goal, however, since gardening is a long-term, constantly developing interest, and one's needs and aims often change over time. The goal is a garden that suits and pleases the owner.

Even if you should decide that your garden needs a complete redesign, before attacking the existing layout, spend a full four seasons watching and taking notes. In this way you can make a complete analysis of the existing landscape's positive and negative features. You can identify which plants are worth saving and which should be replaced, and you'll find the sunniest, most sheltered spot, the one that's ideal for a patio or vegetable garden. Often, aspects of the existing plan can be adapted without a great deal of work or expense — for example, a vista can be screened off or opened up, or the perimeter planting can be adjusted to create an illusion of greater space.

Draw a plan that shows both garden features and existing plants to scale. Before setting spade to soil or removing even one overgrown shrub, plot out all your ideas. It is sensible to establish a basic framework from the beginning, letting the individual features develop over several years. The best plans are those that adapt easily to minor improvements and adjustments as the garden matures and your family's needs change.

Rural haven A tangle of perennials lends this country cottage the perfect air of informal charm.

CREATING AN IDEAL GARDEN

**The style and format of any garden must be tailored
to meet the family's needs and must be
compatible with the architecture of the house.**

There are so many different types of gardens, all beautiful in their own way, that it is easy to be overwhelmed by choice. Not only are there different styles — formal or informal, traditional flower garden or modern, laborsaving layout — there are also hundreds of plants and dozens of garden ornaments available from garden centers and larger discount stores. It isn't, however, simply a matter of choosing attractive plants or bits of outdoor furniture. How the various plants and features are arranged can make the difference between a successful garden — one that is a pleasure to look at and use, as well as easy to maintain — and one that is uninspiring and impractical.

Spending time on working out a good design will save money and labor in the long run by keeping you from making costly mistakes. It is far cheaper to do things once and do them right.

Attention to detail in the planning stage will also ensure that once the landscaping is in place, all areas of the garden will be visually accessible to onlookers and physically accessible to the gardener.

When creating a garden plan, you can choose from numerous styles and countless types of features — patios, rock gardens, pools, rose arbors, or vegetable plots — but take care that they all work together to create a landscape that suits the setting.

A garden is a living thing, and as such it is constantly developing. Whether your garden needs a complete overhaul, a change of design, or just neatening up, there will be plenty to keep you busy.

▲ **Instant gardening** Containers of all kinds, filled with vivid bedding plants, provide instant color to brighten up a garden in the early stages of landscaping or redesign.

▼ **Old-fashioned favorites** Old shrub roses, fast-growing mock orange, lavender, lady's-mantle, and white campanulas seem like old friends in a newly planted property.

▶ **Kitchen garden** A vegetable plot is a must for many gardeners. It should be open to sun and air but can be placed at the property's edge and screened from the main garden with rows of flowers grown especially for cutting.

◀ **Garden pool** Thanks to modern technology, prefabricated pools can be installed in a few hours and filled with flowers and fish within days. But before undertaking such a project, consider how it will fit in with the rest of the design.

▼ **Children's play area** In the outdoor living room, children need a place of their own. Locate sandboxes for toddlers close to the house. Later, you can convert a brick sandbox into a raised planting bed or a small pool.

◀ **Outdoor living space** A backyard patio should be spacious enough to allow for summer meals and entertaining. For convenience, provide free and direct access to the house.

▼ **Vertical emphasis** A rampant *Clematis montana* tumbles over a fence and a house wall, its early-summer pink flowers echoing the warm terra-cotta color of the patio. This exuberant display is countered by the restrained elegance of an urn planted with trailing helichrysum and dainty-leaved, white-flowered marguerites.

Specimen planting Carefully chosen specimen trees create focal points and visual emphasis.

ANALYSIS OF A GARDEN

As the new owner of a garden, take time to assess its character and weigh its strong and weak points before making important changes.

If you know your garden's potential, you can make the most of it, and if you recognize its problems, you can start to correct them. Resist the temptation to begin major improvements and planting programs until you have sorted out your priorities.

If you've just moved into a house, it's a good idea to live with the garden as it is for a year. Fill gaps in the planting with inexpensive bulbs and annuals, while you wait to see what comes up and develop long-term plans. Some professional garden designers find it useful to take photographs to help them see (and remember) a garden as it really is. You can build a visual reference file by taking photographs from one position, such as the center of the lawn, and other shots from the rooms in your house that overlook the garden. Take photographs in all the seasons, even winter.

Existing plants

Established trees and shrubs give a garden character, a feeling of permanence and privacy. If planted in an inconvenient spot, smaller specimens can often be transplanted during their dormant season without too much trouble. Others that seem too big or are overgrown or misshapen can often be improved by drastic pruning.

Think twice about removing mature trees; the loss of shade and shelter will affect the garden's microclimate as well as its appearance. Discuss the decision with an arborist, as this job is best left to a professional anyway. Remember that if you change your mind afterward, it will take years to grow a new tree.

Vistas and eyesores

A pleasant view from the garden of a distant or nearby scene is worth "framing" with upright trees or shrubs on either side. Site a garden seat to face the view, or redirect a path toward it.

Eyesores within the garden — such as a garage, shed, or compost pile — can be camouflaged with climbers or dense-growing shrubs. Eyesores outside the garden are more difficult to hide; you may

▲ **Visual evidence** For a panoramic record of the garden, take several photographs from the same spot, turning with your camera to capture the whole expanse.

need to plant fast-growing trees or install a wooden trellis or other type of privacy screen.

Evergreens provide a complete year-round screen but may also block out too much light. Deciduous plants are a good compromise: they offer reasonable screening but let in light in winter, when light levels are low.

Soil

The type of soil in your garden — whether heavy, sticky clay or silt;

Focal points Emphasize an attractive distant view by framing it with trees, an arch, or a pergola. Or site a garden seat or direct a path so that the eye is guided toward the view.

Screening eyesores A hedge or fence can conceal necessary but unattractive objects. This frees the rest of the garden for an attractive layout and ornamental features.

▶ **Distant vista** Grand planting schemes can be adapted in scale to suit smaller gardens. This geometric design is based on a straight path of granite paving stones leading to a circular platform with a huge urn as a centerpiece against a backdrop of blue-flowered ceanothus. The surrounding beds of annual flowers, edged with low clipped boxwood, serve to reinforce the view of the urn from a distance.

▼ **Enclosed vista** A gravel-covered driveway enclosed by large mature trees has a striking focal point — a large terra-cotta jar containing an arching phoenix palm, with a cluster of bright nasturtiums at its base. Even on a cloudy day, the pale-colored gravel appears as a pool of light.

light, well-drained, sandy soil; a rich loam; or a mixture of these types — doesn't really affect the layout of the garden. However, certain plants require certain soils — azaleas and rhododendrons, for example, thrive only on well-drained acid soil — so it is wise to match plants to soil type from the outset.

Most plants, notably perennials and annuals, will grow in a wide range of soils. And while you cannot change a soil type, you can greatly improve its overall structure and texture.

Sun and shade

The pattern of sun and shade in a garden varies according to the time of day and the time of year. Certain spots may get morning sun; others, afternoon or evening sun; and still others, no direct sun at all. Once again, a few photographs taken at different times of day and year will reveal the changing patterns of light and shade. Some plants are equally happy in sun or light shade; others are more choosy.

There's nothing you can do to alter shade from buildings, walls, and north-facing slopes, but trees can often be pruned to allow more sunlight into the garden. Shady spots are often dry, because whatever blocks out light also prevents rain from getting in.

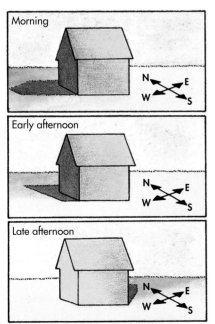

Sun and shade Light levels change depending on the time of day. In the morning the sun is in the east, shading the west and northwest sides of a house. As the sun gradually moves westward, the east and northeast sides start to go into shadow.

Exposure

A garden set on a south-facing slope warms up earlier in spring than a similar garden on level ground. During the cold winter months, a north-facing slope is hardly touched at all by the sun's low rays.

Exposure will obviously affect where you put particular plants. Sun-loving plants will never succeed in a very shady site.

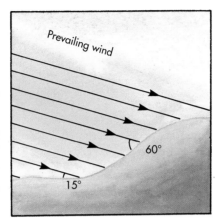

South-facing slopes These absorb more of the sun's heat than level ground does, so that temperatures are higher, especially in areas sheltered from wind.

Local weather conditions

How cold it gets in winter, how hot in summer, and the dates of the first and last frosts vary from one part of the country to another. What's more, conditions vary somewhat each year and are affected by the lay of the land; a valley tends to be warmer in summer than a nearby hill, but in winter the reverse may be true. Rainfall also will vary, but watering can make up the difference.

Some plants are hardier than others, so bear in mind the local climate when choosing permanent plants and timing the sowing of summer beds and vegetables.

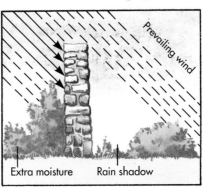

Walls, hedges, and fences These create dry areas on the leeward side of the prevailing wind, so plants sited there will need extra watering.

Wind and windbreaks

Plants do not like wind, which can be drying or chilling, and often both. Strong wind can also break off branches and even loosen plants' roots, which will eventually kill them.

Walls provide shelter but, depending on where they are sited, can also create unwanted shade and wind turbulence. Partial screening, in the form of hedges, fences, or trellises, is often a better choice. The wind is then filtered through the fence or hedge and its force reduced without buffeting plants sited nearby.

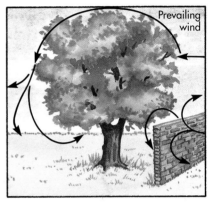

Wind barriers Solid walls, buildings, and dense trees block the wind, causing turbulence on the leeward side.

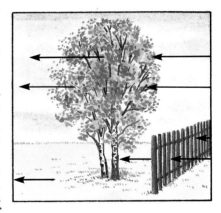

Wind filters Fences and light trees allow wind to pass through, reducing its intensity without causing turbulence.

Other man-made features

A new garden that includes a large outbuilding, such as a garage, must be designed around that feature. Paths and gates, as well as smaller features such as birdbaths, can be moved, replaced, or removed to improve the look and organization of the garden.

You'll know if a hard-surfaced path is in the wrong place — a worn-out patch of lawn nearby will show you a better location for it.

Choosing garden features

There is no one special recipe for creating the perfect garden, although there are useful guidelines for choosing and combining the different features found in most people's gardens. Initially, it is partly a matter of striking a balance between too many features, which can make a garden seem busy, and too few, which make a garden seem boring or unfinished. In addition, it is a matter of making the garden and house work comfortably together. Most important, the finished garden should reflect your personal taste and style.

In analyzing your garden, consider the unalterable factors of property lines, exposure, soil type, and local climate. These are the foundations upon which you must create your garden. For the best results, think positively; regard whatever obstacles you find as challenges that can be overcome rather than as insoluble problems.

Getting started

The following descriptions of screens and dividers, planting features, and leisure and decorative features is an at-a-glance guide to the main elements that go into creating a garden. Don't try to incorporate them all. After installing one feature, live with it awhile before moving on to the next project. Start by reading through the list, and relate the features to your garden both as it is now and as you want it to be.

Making your own list of all the features will help you if you're not sure where or how to start. As you do so, note which features your garden already has that you want to:
- ❏ Retain
- ❏ Improve
- ❏ Add
- ❏ Remove

Then pause for thought and consider whether you are trying to cram in too much.

Next, decide which features on your list are essential, which are desirable, and which you could do without. This step is especially helpful if, like most people, you can't create your ideal garden all at once and instead have to proceed with the project in stages.

SCREENS AND DIVIDERS

These form the boundary to a garden or divide it into a series of different "rooms." Depending on the need, these can be high or low, stretching right across the garden or only a part of it.

Walls

A brick or stone wall is durable and attractive. It offers a sense of privacy and creates a warm, sheltered microclimate that is ideal for tender plants or for sitting. A wall used to retain soil in a sloping site establishes a change in level.

New walls are very expensive to build and can look raw to start with. Walls of decorative concrete block are an attractive, economical, but less durable alternative to brick and stone. In any case, choose a material that suits the style of your house.

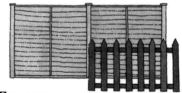

Fences

Fences are cheaper than walls and need less skill to erect. They offer instant enclosure and come in a wide range of materials, from solid or woven wood panels to open wire mesh.

Most fences need regular maintenance or occasional replacement. Climbing plants can hide plain fences but may make fence maintenance difficult.

Hedges

Established hedges are attractive and make a restful background for other plants. Some hedging plants grow slowly; those that grow quickly often take over available space. Most need regular pruning. Hedges take up more space than walls and use nutrients and water from the soil.

Paths

Paths should be firm, easy to walk on, generously wide, and fast draining. The material should complement the house and other hard surfaces, such as a nearby patio or steps.

Path layouts should relate to the house, garage doors, and garden gates. Paths that wander aimlessly are rarely used.

Level changes

Slopes, retaining walls, and raised beds or even sunken patios make a garden interesting and provide homes for rock or alpine plants.

Steps should be firm, dry, and evenly spaced, complementing nearby paving.

MAIN PLANT FEATURES

If well coordinated, the plantings knit together to make the garden attractive throughout the year.

Grass

Lawns provide good surfaces for play and a calm setting for flower beds or other colorful displays. Starting from seed is inexpensive; laying sod is expensive but "instant." A rougher, meadowlike lawn can be effective in large gardens, reducing the need for mowing and offering a home to wildflowers and bulbs.

Lawns do not flourish in dense shade or areas of heavy foot traffic. Formal lawns need regular mowing and trimming through spring, summer, and fall — and winter, too, in the deep south.

Flowers

Herbaceous perennials, biennials, annuals, and bulbs are all types of plants that can provide quick color interest for both new and established gardens.

You can afford to be adventurous with these plants because most can easily be moved and rearranged if you find yourself dissatisfied with your initial plan or if you wish a different effect.

Shrubs

Shrubs bring a feeling of depth and space to a garden, making a flat rectangle of ground seem more interesting or larger than it really is. They also add height and texture to a mixed border and serve as a perfect foil for annuals and perennials.

Shrub and mixed borders generally work best when they are 3-6 ft (90-180 cm) wide. When narrower, the plants tend to run out of growing room; if made wider, the border is difficult to cultivate.

Trees

Trees, more than any other feature, make a garden look established and give it a three-dimensional quality.

Because today's gardens are likely to be small, nurseries and garden centers offer many ornamental trees that will grow no taller at maturity (about 20 years) than 23-26 ft (7-8 m).

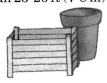

Containers

Plant containers are perfect for adding spots of color to a garden. They are available in a wide range of sizes, materials, shapes, and styles.

Larger containers are more effective and require watering less often. They are also less likely to be knocked over. For outdoor use, choose containers of plastic or wood that can withstand frost.

SPECIALIZED PLANTINGS

Even the smallest garden can accommodate an enthusiasm for a special kind of plant.

Rose gardens

Everybody loves roses, and many gardeners devote entire beds to the hybrid teas and floribundas, which can flower from early summer to late fall. Most roses prefer sun and rich, slightly heavy, well-drained soil, but some will flower reasonably well in light shade.

Old garden roses have better-looking foliage and forms — and more interesting hips — than modern types. Think about how a rose bed will look while it is in bloom; consider low underplanting and evergreen edging for the dreary winter months.

Rock gardens

Rock gardens provide the perfect setting for attractive alpine plants, as well as dwarf conifers. For the most natural appearance,

use local rocks of the same type and avoid rounded glacial boulders. Rock gardens look best on slopes — they rarely seem natural in flat areas. Growing alpine plants in raised beds or trough gardens is a popular alternative.

Heather beds

With their evergreen foliage and flowers, which range from white through pink and lavender to deepest purple, heathers can brighten a garden year-round.

Newly planted heather beds need regular weeding until the plants mat together. For added interest, include a few dwarf conifers or rhododendrons.

Vegetables

Growing your own vegetables saves money and provides tasty fresh produce.

You don't need a separate area for growing vegetables. Many, including runner beans and loose-leaf lettuce, are decorative enough to be grown among flowers and shrubs in mixed borders or in large pots.

Fruit

Fruit trees can be as ornamental as they are practical, providing flowers, fall leaf color, and winter interest as well as delicious crops.

For small gardens, fruit trees on dwarfing rootstocks are best. Trees trained as espaliers, fans, or cordons can be grown flat against a wall or a sturdy wooden fence. Most fruit trees need a mate of the right type nearby for cross-pollination; check with the nursery before you buy.

Herbs

Herbs can be grown successfully in mixed borders, containers, or window boxes, as well as in traditional herb gardens.

When harvesting herbs for the kitchen, pick just a few leaves at a time. Completely stripping a plant may kill it.

LEISURE FEATURES

These are as important as plants if you and your family want to relax in the garden.

Patios and paved areas

Ideally, a patio should be sheltered and sunny for a good bit of the day and have an attractive view or a cozy, self-contained feel. All paved

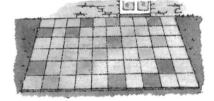

areas should be securely laid, level, as well as fast draining, and the paving should match nearby hard surfaces.

The closer a patio is to a house, the better. Make sure it's large enough for a suitable table and chairs. To decorate the patio area, arrange plants in tubs and large flowerpots.

Furniture

Well-chosen and well-positioned furniture can transform a garden into a pleasant room for outdoor living and entertaining. Fixed garden furniture should be heavy, durable, and weatherproof. Movable garden furniture should be stable but light enough to be carried easily.

Too much furniture in a garden makes it look like a garden center. Instead, choose a few comfortable pieces of good quality. Keep in mind, too, that movable outdoor furniture requires indoor space for winter storage. If space is limited, choose chairs that can be stacked.

Barbecues

Barbecues are focal points for family meals as well as entertaining. Built-in barbecues are expensive but worthwhile if used often. Portable ones are more flexible and can be stored in the winter.

For safety, site the barbecue on level ground away from paths and overhanging trees — especially hollies and conifers.

Children's play areas

Young children need a sheltered, sunny place to play within sight of the house. Older children prefer some privacy and would enjoy

climbing bars or a swing hidden behind a privacy screen.

Swings and slides must be well anchored in the ground and have a soft surface, such as loose sand (not grass, which quickly wears away with use), underneath.

DECORATIVE FEATURES

These provide focal points and express a garden's personality.

Garden pools

With its water plants, fish, and reflections, an ornamental pool makes an instant focal point. Most are now made of rigid fiberglass or flexible polyethylene, PVC, or rubber sheeting and come in many colors, shapes, and sizes. Generally, simple shapes look more natural than complicated ones.

A sunny, open, level site away from overhanging trees is ideal. Ornamental pools need cleaning out from time to time.

For safety's sake, children must be supervised around uncovered pools. Tragic pool accidents can happen all too quickly.

Before you install a garden pool, check with your local building department or other authorized local official for safety and building code requirements.

Arches and pergolas

These add instant height to a garden and can emphasize an entrance or a view. They are ideal for climbing plants and can be iron,

brick, aluminum, wood, or a combination of materials.

Arches and pergolas look most effective linking other features (such as a hedge) rather than standing by themselves.

Statues and ornaments

A statue, birdbath, or sundial can contribute that special something to a garden.

Try not to get carried away and buy too many ornaments, as the effect can be very busy. Making a focal point of a sundial and putting a statue in an enclosed corner so that the viewer comes upon it as a surprise are two effective ideas.

Choose these ornaments with

care — they will adorn your garden for years to come.

BUILDINGS

The best garden buildings are attractive as well as functional.

Greenhouses

These are places for growing potted plants for the house or seedlings for the garden. They can also be used to display plants. You can choose from a wide range of ready-made models, but all need a sunny, sheltered site.

The most common mistake is to

buy a greenhouse that is too small. Smaller structures are more expensive to heat per unit of growing space.

Sheds and summerhouses

These, too, are available ready-made or prefabricated in a range of materials, sizes, and prices. If you already have an unattractive garden building, you can either paint it or cover it with a suitable, vigorous climber.

LAYING OUT A GARDEN

**Every garden contains a number of ornamental
and practical features — the trick is arranging them
to appear completely harmonious.**

Placing features in your garden is much like arranging furniture in your living room — there is no right or wrong way, just what is most practical and attractive for you and your family.

Unlike room furniture, however, many garden features are difficult to shift once in position — paths and ornamental pools are examples. Others, such as shrubs and trees, really don't appreciate being moved once they've settled in. That's why it pays to think through all the options ahead of time.

Traditional layouts

The traditional approach, illustrated in the sample garden at right, runs along straight, symmetrical lines. Flower and shrub borders flank the sides of the garden, and a path runs down the center. Utilitarian areas are reserved for either end of the rectangle: a vegetable patch and a greenhouse at the far end, a paved seating area and a toolshed near the house.

Every feature is treated as worthy of display, as a sculpture is in a museum. Each element is given equal importance and space to walk around, so the garden becomes a showcase.

While each element can be appreciated on its own, this approach can give a garden an uncoordinated, fragmented look. And because of the layout, the whole garden can be seen and absorbed at once, leaving the visitor no element of suspense.

What this garden lacks is a sense of depth. By arranging the features in clusters or groups, you can make the same space seem bigger and more exciting. Changes in level and varying the height of features introduce a

welcome element of surprise, and by interrupting views, you keep visitors from discovering the whole garden at once. Instead, they must explore along paths and around corners to uncover the pleasures of your garden.

Suggesting depth

Some gardens have a built-in feeling of depth — large country gardens, for example — with major trees as part of the scene and views to distant fields, villages, or

hills. But how do you set about creating a feeling of depth in a smaller garden?

Begin by enclosing the garden. You could use a solid boundary, such as a high wall, or a partial shield, perhaps a light fence. Try thinking of your garden as a theater stage where you are arranging the scenery. To break up the view, use a few large, simple features — some shrubs, big pots, a hedge or a trellis, a few clumps of pampas grass, or an arbor. Place

Traditional garden A typical layout is based on straight lines within which the various garden features are displayed one by one. The functional design is uninspiring, but a little creative imagination can transform it.

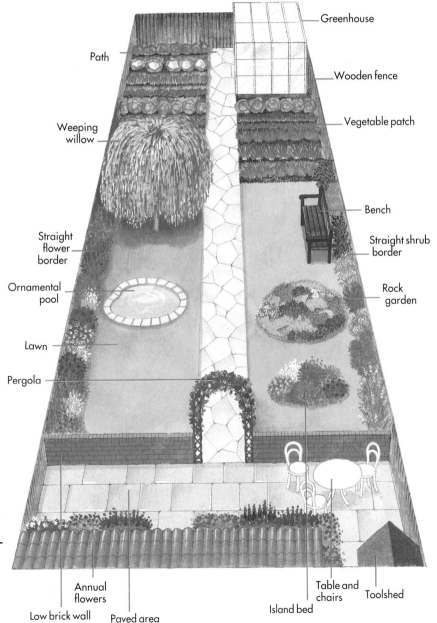

Greenhouse

Path

Wooden fence

Weeping willow

Vegetable patch

Bench

Straight flower border

Straight shrub border

Ornamental pool

Rock garden

Lawn

Pergola

Annual flowers

Table and chairs

Toolshed

Low brick wall

Paved area

Island bed

this "scenery" in the foreground, jutting out from the side of the garden or stretching across the width, with a pergola in the center to provide a passageway and frame the view beyond.

Small gardens probably have room for only a single interruption — avoid cramming in too many features. Larger gardens, especially long ones, can hold several. These divide the garden into a number of separate spaces, each with a different feature or focal point.

Varying the height

Most people design their gardens with the tallest plants — trees — near the back, medium-height

GIVING THE GARDEN DEPTH

View from the house
1 Use a piece of cardboard to represent the area of the garden, cutting it to match its actual shape. Imagine your viewpoint to be straight down the garden from the house. The idea is to build gradually on this surface, using a variety of features to create interesting spaces and focal points.

2 Even the largest gardens benefit from some sense of enclosure, and in small gardens it can make all the difference. As well as screening less attractive nearby views and furnishing privacy, enclosures define the perimeters and provide an empty "stage" on which to arrange and rearrange the scenery.

3 Large, simple features can break up the central space in a garden and give your imagination room to play. Remember that the closer an object is to you, the more elements it will hide from view. Here, an evergreen hedge, ending in a pergola, creates a sense of anticipation and mystery, tempting you to approach and look around the corner.

4 The addition of a second hedge and a tree at the far end leads the eye from one space to the next by setting up a series of receding areas.

Because the eye has distances to measure, a feeling of depth is created. You can imagine yourself looking through the pergola and wondering what features might be hidden beyond the hedge.

5 Breaking up a single space into smaller areas often leads to further changes. Here, different surface materials emphasize the separate divisions, and the paving-stone path is given a real reason to curve on its journey to the bench at the far end. But all you can see initially is the hedge and a planted container.

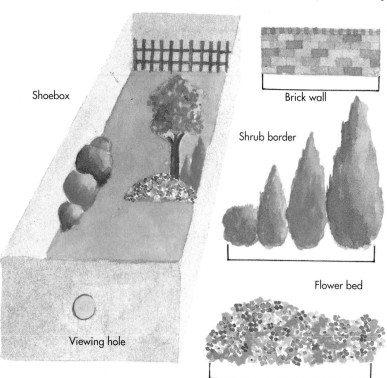

Shoebox

Viewing hole

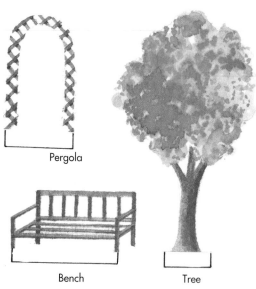

Brick wall

Shrub border

Pergola

Flower bed

Bench

Tree

Use a shoebox to represent the garden, and cut out cardboard shapes for the chosen features. These need only be simple silhouettes with a right-angle fold at the base. Looking through the viewing hole — which corresponds to eye height — try out different permutations.

▶ Curves and depth
Flowing curves create pockets of mystery in this garden. From the paved area, where a small statue marks the transition into greenery, the upper part of the shrubbery is hidden from view, while at the other end a trellis with climbers offers a tantalizing glimpse of a secluded sitting area.

Curves visually increase the size of the garden and invite closer inspection of the mysteries hidden behind the semicircular planting bed.

▼ Hidden retreats A pergola clothed with fast-growing ivies and honeysuckle frames the entrance to a sunny concealed court. Velvety grass gives way to mellow stone, punctuated with weathered pots of impatiens. Beyond lies a sheet of gravel.

plants — shrubs — in the middle, and bedding plants toward the front. This is one way of giving the garden height. An alternative approach is to bring some taller plants forward to break up the outline.

Tall elements at the back make a garden look shorter; tall features close to the house make a garden look longer. Choose trees carefully: their shapes, outlines, foliage, flowers (if any), and ultimate size. Large forest trees are inappropriate for most gardens.

Varying the height of plants and other features has the same effect as adding depth: it gradually leads the eye through the length of the garden. Tall plants act as visual exclamation points, contrasting with lower ones.

Changing the level

Level changes increase the appeal of a garden — a low level with a secluded feeling can rise to give a sense of openness. Rural

---

▼ **Height and space** Varying the height of trees and shrubs, from creeping conifers to slender columnar types, gives an impression of space.

ADDING HEIGHT

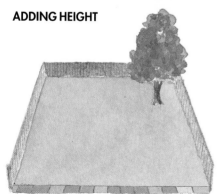

View from the house
1 One good-size tree is the key to making height work for you in a garden. The tree becomes a focal point, drawing the eye down the length of the garden.

2 A shrub about 4 ft (1.2 m) high at the front or halfway down the garden adds contrast and gives the eye something to measure the tree against — a sort of bouncing-off point.

3 Before planting any trees, be sure to check the ultimate size. Ask the nursery the height and spread after 15 years. Compact species may grow no taller than 25 ft (7.5 m).

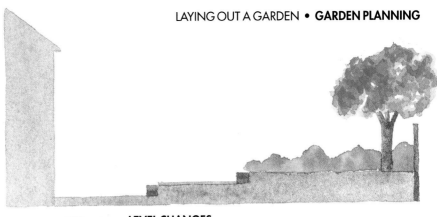

and suburban gardens are likely to retain the natural slope or contours of the land, while gardens of older urban houses may have a sunken area outside the back door with steps leading up to the rest of the garden.

Rather than treating existing level changes as a problem, make them a feature. Changing the surface texture of each level — from paving to grass, for example — defines the divisions and gives each a different purpose.

Making level changes in a flat garden requires careful thought. Most levels immediately outside a house can't be adjusted without affecting the drainage of water away from the foundation. Away from the house, you can take earth from one part of the garden — lowering the level there — and use it to raise the level somewhere else. Raised planting beds are one possibility and informally curved planting mounds another.

Rearranging a garden
Compare the garden on page 24 with the diagram on page 19, and

LEVEL CHANGES
The cross section (above) and frontal view (left) show how you can give character to a garden by splitting it into three levels. Each level is defined by altering the surface material. Here, the terracing has been accomplished inexpensively using the "cut and fill" method: soil removed from the lower areas was used to level higher ones. This eliminates the need for new soil (buying new soil of good quality, especially topsoil, may be expensive). It is important, when building up soil levels next to a boundary wall or fence, to make sure the wall is strong enough to take the additional pressure.

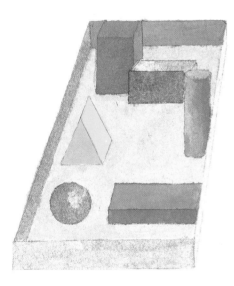

▶ **Low retaining walls** are well within the ability of many do-it-yourselfers and increase the range of design possibilities in a garden.

▼ **A change in level** here gives emphasis to the focal point — a circular bench enclosing a fruit tree.

▲ **Heights and levels** In the lid of a box, arrange children's building blocks in various patterns, imagining them as different-size plants. It will help you to work out how to arrange the varying heights of trees, shrubs, and bedding plants and to visualize how the bulk of several will look if set close together. Because the blocks have simple shapes and don't look like particular plants, you won't get sidetracked into thinking about the flowers or leaves. An oblong laid flat serves a dual purpose: it can represent either a flower bed or a raised level. Remember to lower your head so that eye level is just above the rim of the lid; the idea is to look through the blocks, not down on them.

you will see that the same basic features appear in both, on a site of identical shape and size. In the version on this page, the features have been arranged to make the best use of depth, height, and level changes. The result is a clear expanse of lawn, easy to maintain and restful to the eye, and a series of spaces and features that lead the eye from one to another.

Near the house a rose-covered pergola frames the view of the garden, focusing the eye on a birdbath at the other end of the path. The pergola creates an impressive entrance into the main garden and links the raised shrub beds, which make the patio more sheltered and secluded.

The slightly raised sitting area and raised beds transform a flat garden into one with three levels,

and the nearby tree and pergola provide variation in height. The hedge helps to conceal the greenhouse and vegetable patch and prevents the entire garden from being seen at once, thus helping to give a feeling of depth and size.

A curving border filled with mixed perennial and annual flowers softens the long, straight lines of the garden's boundary fence and of the path, which remains unchanged, since it follows the shortest route down the garden. The combination of rock garden and nearby pool makes a year-round focal point and helps to disguise the garden's long linear shape.

Initial planning
Most gardens consist of a lawn, beds and borders, a patio, and

CHECKLIST

The following are used in the layout on page 19 and the reorganized version below. Not listed here is the hedge, a feature new to the "second" garden.
Flower beds
Flower border
Lawn
Rock garden
Shrubbery
Specimen tree
Vegetable patch
Greenhouse
Fence
Low wall
Path
Patio
Pergola
Ornamental pool
Seating
Toolshed

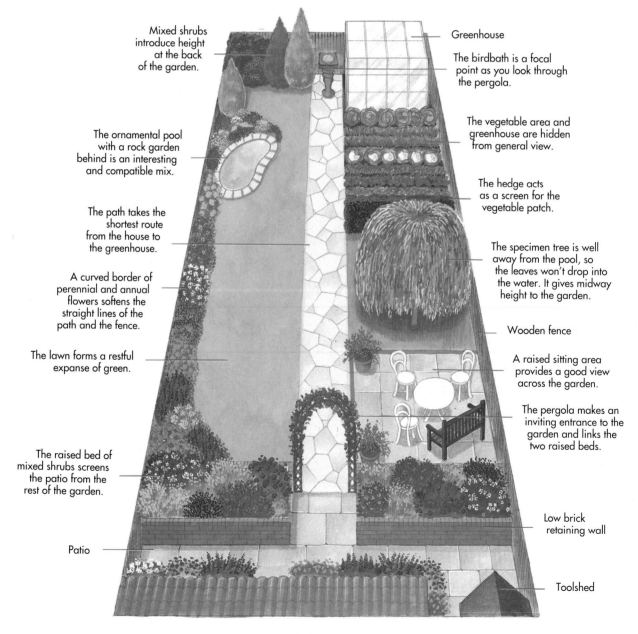

Mixed shrubs introduce height at the back of the garden.

Greenhouse

The birdbath is a focal point as you look through the pergola.

The vegetable area and greenhouse are hidden from general view.

The ornamental pool with a rock garden behind is an interesting and compatible mix.

The hedge acts as a screen for the vegetable patch.

The path takes the shortest route from the house to the greenhouse.

The specimen tree is well away from the pool, so the leaves won't drop into the water. It gives midway height to the garden.

A curved border of perennial and annual flowers softens the straight lines of the path and the fence.

Wooden fence

A raised sitting area provides a good view across the garden.

The lawn forms a restful expanse of green.

The pergola makes an inviting entrance to the garden and links the two raised beds.

The raised bed of mixed shrubs screens the patio from the rest of the garden.

Low brick retaining wall

Patio

Toolshed

HOUSE

such major features as a pool or a rock garden. In addition, there are useful service areas, such as the compost pile, toolshed, and greenhouse. Few gardeners can afford to install all these components immediately, but you need to allocate space for each in the initial layout so that they can be added as your budget and time permit.

Where you are creating a new garden from a bare plot, you will probably have a fairly free hand in evolving your personal style. Established gardens can be difficult to transform, and you may be compelled to retain certain features and adapt or remove others before the backbone of the new garden begins to emerge.

The first step in garden planning is usually locating the patio or deck, which should be in scale with the house and easily accessible. Once you have sited this outdoor living room, the rest of the garden framework can be related to it, and the shape of beds and borders will often emerge as a matter of course.

Making a plan
Drawing up a plan will help you to think of the garden as a whole unit, not just a collection of flower beds, paths, lawn, and shrubs. It also forces you to think about the long-term look of the garden, in addition to instant improvements. With a plan, you can proceed in an orderly way, as and when funds and time allow.

Before deciding on the final design, sketch several possible layouts, retaining existing features that you want to keep or trying new ones and concealing or removing eyesores. Trial and error on paper costs virtually nothing. Mistakes can literally be thrown away, so be adventurous.

Make a sketch of the existing garden on plain paper attached to a clipboard. Sketch the boundaries and general shape in freehand. Viewing the garden from an upstairs window helps; so does pacing the distances, using your normal stride as a unit of measurement. Moving around while you sketch gives a clearer picture of where things are than if you work solely from, say, the kitchen window.

Draw in the house walls, marking windows and doors. Indicate trees, including the ones that overhang from next door; paths; walls and level changes; beds; patios or decks; sheds; lawns; ornaments; and fixed play equipment.

Note other important information, such as the prevailing wind direction, where north is, sunny and shady spots, and good and bad views.

Measuring
On the sketch, draw dimension lines along the boundaries of the garden. If it is four-sided but not square or rectangular, draw two diagonals to fix the exact angles of the corners. Similarly, if the garden has a complicated form, divide it into simpler, easily measurable shapes that converge.

Use a surveyor's tape measure or a length of string with knots at measured intervals. With a helper to hold one end of the tape or string, measure each dimension line on the ground and record each length on the sketch.

Using a corner of the house as a fixed point, you can extend a parallel line down the length of the garden, then plot more positions, such as a nearby path or tree, by taking offset measurements at 90° angles from the main line (shown as dotted lines below). To locate complicated positions, use triangulation (see box on page 26).

▼ **Drawing to scale** A rough sketch of an existing garden should incorporate all fixtures and planting areas, whether or not you wish to retain them.

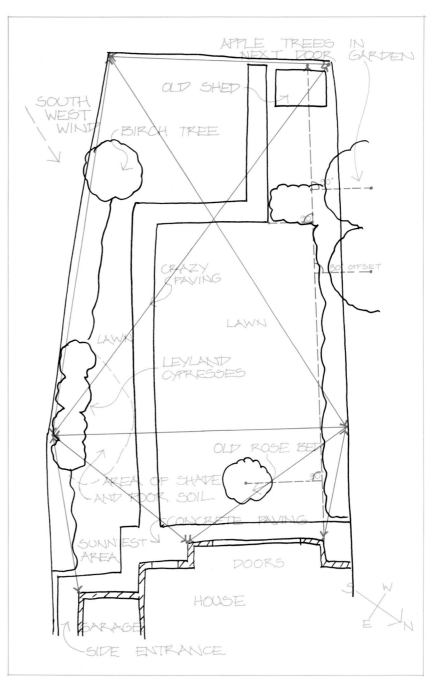

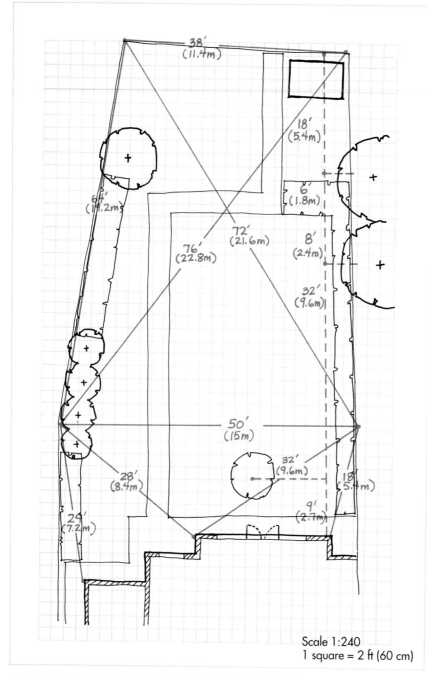

38'
(11.4m)

18'
(5.4m)

6'
(1.8m)

6'
(1.2m)

72'
(21.6m)

76'
(22.8m)

8'
(2.4m)

32'
(9.6m)

50'
(15m)

32'
(9.6m)

18'
(5.4m)

28'
(8.4m)

9'
(2.7m)

24'
(7.2m)

Scale 1:240
1 square = 2 ft (60 cm)

◄ **Graph plan** To make an accurately scaled plan, transfer the rough sketch of the garden to graph paper. If necessary, certain areas can be studied further by pulling them out and enlarging the scale to see them in more detail.

Transferring the sketch

Make the final copy on graph paper with 10 squares per inch, choosing a scale and paper size that allows the garden to fit on one sheet. For smaller gardens, a scale of 1:120 is best; each square on the paper will equal a 1 ft (30 cm) square on the ground.

Average gardens may be drawn to a scale of 1:240, in which each square on the paper equals a 2 ft (60 cm) square on the ground. Large gardens can be drawn on two sheets of graph paper taped together or drawn to a smaller scale, with sections drawn again to 1:120 (one square=1 ft/30 cm). Work out details at 1:60 (one square=6 in/15 cm).

Check first that the two widest dimensions on the rough sketch will fit on the graph paper at the intended scale, leaving a margin around the actual plan.

In most instances, it is best to start by drawing the house dimensions, then work outward from these fixed points to the boundaries and various features, either by triangulation or 90° offset readings. Use a no. 2 pencil and a metal straightedge to get a clear, sharp drawing, and use a compass for the triangulation method.

Plotting the layout

Tape tracing paper over the scaled plan, then mark on it those features, such as a shed or a tree, that you want or have to keep. Next, look at the remaining space in terms of a few simple, large geometric shapes, such as squares and rectangles. Use the basic shape of the garden as a starting point, repeating any attractive curves or angles on a smaller scale.

The smaller the garden, the simpler the layout should be. In time, plants will soften harsh edges and make shapes less obvious. Intricate layouts may look interesting on paper but often look confused on the ground and are difficult to maintain.

Balance colorful planting areas with visually restful ones, such as

Triangulation

To find the exact position of a feature that is difficult to locate by 90° offset readings (previous page), measure it from any two fixed points. Some examples are at right:
1) To plot path corner, measure from that spot to two nearby house corners.
2) To plot rosebush position, measure from that spot to house and to path corner.
3) To plot cypress tree at rear of garden, measure from that spot to path corner and bush.

On the final drawing, use a compass, set to the right distance according to the scale, to make intersecting arcs that pinpoint the spot.

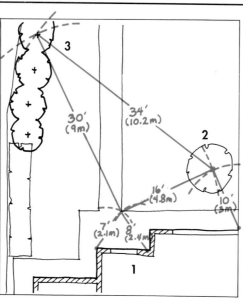

3

30'
(9m)

34'
(10.2m)

2

16'
(4.8m)

10'
(3m)

7'
(2.1m)

8'
(2.4m)

1

a lawn; colored pencils or felt-tip markers can help you work out the design. Think about introducing level changes — a raised planting bed or a sunken pool complete with sloping rock garden, for instance — if the garden is totally flat.

Work from a checklist of the features you want to include and list them in order of priority. As you position each one, consider whether it is best set in sun or shade, in full view or hidden, near the house or far away, and so on. As a general rule, it is easier to correct and improve an existing layout than to design it from scratch, especially for the beginner.

Remember to mark on the plan any utility boxes, drains, and gas and water lines, all of which can determine the siting of

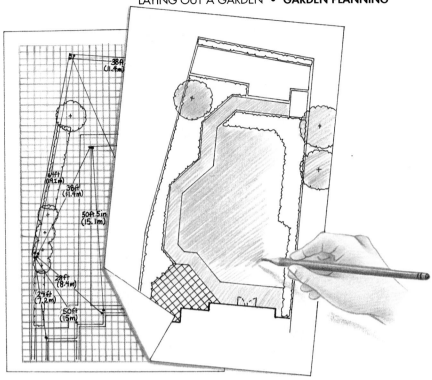

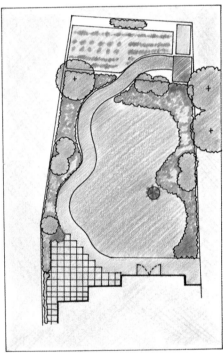

▲ **Planning the design** Having transferred the shape of the garden to graph paper, lay tracing paper over the top and try out different plans to work out the best design. First include features that are staying put, such as trees, since these limit and affect the rest of the layout. Then decide how to arrange other features in the most practical and attractive way.

◄ **Perspective** Although a plan to be used for garden installation must be drawn in two dimensions, as if seen from overhead, depth and height changes spring to life only in a three-dimensional plan. A useful last step in the design process is to draw a three-dimensional perspective, as at left.

plants and fixtures. Put the plan aside for a few days, then look at it again with fresh eyes and make alterations at this stage or draw a completely new plan.

Making a long-term plan

It isn't realistic to create mature lawns and plants, paving, and features all within the first year. Budgets are often limited and the work is usually extensive. Fortunately, an unfinished garden can still be attractive, and with a list of priorities and a sensible schedule, you will likely save time, money, and effort.

Begin the project by removing unwanted items, then work on the framework of the garden. Make major level changes, if necessary, and fix the position of the paths, patio, cold frames, and greenhouse, even if you can't construct them yet. Enclose the perimeter, as planned, for security and privacy.

Give priority to establishing large, long-term plants, such as trees, followed by shrubs and climbers and, finally, perennials, bulbs, and annuals.

A few trays of bedding plants can brighten up a first-year garden, and it doesn't matter where you put them, as they only last one season. Large flowerpots and tubs are always useful, since they can be instantly filled with plants and moved around to wherever color is needed.

Ornamental features, such as pools, rock gardens, and pergolas, can be constructed after the main planting and garden framework are established — but remember to set aside the space.

▼ **Small and perfect** However well planned, a garden develops gradually. Only as plants mature and fill out do the creative merits of the design become apparent.

PLANT MATERIAL

Creative garden designs use a variety of plants to maintain color and focal interest all year round.

Many new gardeners put their efforts and money into a colorful summer display and forget about the other months of the year. A good garden design uses plants for year-round effect, creating areas of seasonal interest and relying on permanent and evergreen groups to keep the garden alive when herbaceous plants have died down for their winter rest.

A balance of plants

The garden featured on the following pages shows how to enjoy a summer crescendo of color and still have plenty of interest during the rest of the year.

The garden faces west and thus has summer sun most of the day; gardens with less favorable aspects can be equally stunning, for many bedding plants do well in dappled shade.

The recipe for year-round success is simple for any garden: include a balance of plants. Mix short-lived seasonal plants with permanent trees and shrubs, deciduous with evergreen, flowers with foliage, strong colors with green or similar soothing hues. Also, balance masses with well-placed focal points.

Seasonal planting

Marking the progress of the year with seasonal planting is a great pleasure in gardening, and many people spend the winter browsing through seed catalogs, choosing new varieties and colors.

▲ **Summer highlights** In this mature garden, borders of shrubs and foliage plants form props for a velvety lawn and island beds of brilliant flowers.

▼ **Raised beds** Level changes in steps and raised beds brimming with color-coordinated upright, trailing, and climbing plants bring a three-dimensional feeling to this paved patio.

Growing your own bedding plants from seed is economical — particularly if you are planning a display on the scale of this garden — but you can find yourself swamped with unwanted plants.

If you need only a relatively small number of plants, buy them ready-grown in late spring. Larger garden centers generally feature a number of unusual varieties among the standbys.

Raised beds built into the patio contain bedding plants. Each bed has its own color theme and particular plants and patterns. One bed displays pink petunias, blue lobelias, and white alyssums; another puts on a striking show of red-purple lobelias, yellow bedding calceolarias, white alyssums, and pink geraniums.

Containers on the patio also have color themes. Bright red begonias, both tuberous-rooted and wax types, fill the two-level stone container, while trailing fuchsias, alyssums, geraniums *(Pelargonium)*, *Helichrysum petiolatum*, and lobelias are combined in urns and rectangular planters.

Two island beds in the lawn are filled with more fuchsias — shrubby types for bulk and standards for height. The beds are edged with impatiens and begonias in shades of red.

Every fall the beds and containers are cleared and prepared for the following spring's display.

The fuchsias are dug up and then overwintered in the frost-free greenhouse. The tuberous-rooted begonias are lifted, dried off, and overwintered in boxes of dry potting mix.

Geranium cuttings are taken to start plants for the next summer's display, and annuals are added to the compost pile to rot into humus, which will restore to the soil the nutrients the petunias removed over a summer's growth.

Spring bedding includes numerous tulips and daffodils. This is not as extravagant as it seems, since many bulbs last for years if properly looked after. Early in the summer, when flowering has finished and the foliage has yellowed, the bedding tulips are lifted, cleaned, and dried off, then replanted during the fall. Daffodils and narcissi can stay in the ground, unless (as here) the beds are dug up for summer bedding.

Young bulblets produced by the parent bulbs are set out in a nursery area to grow on for 2 or 3 years until they are big enough to flower heavily, increasing the bulbs at no cost to the gardener.

Biennials, such as wallflowers, pansies, forget-me-nots, sweet Williams, primroses, and English daisies, are set out as seedlings in fall to bloom the following spring and summer. Grown from seed sown the previous spring, these flowers perform like hardy annuals in this garden's mild climate, growing right through the winter to bloom far earlier than bedding plants set out in springtime.

Permanent planting

Adequate space is given to long-term residents — trees, shrubs, and a selection of conifers — which provide the permanent setting for the changing spring and summer displays. They reduce considerably the amount of maintenance needed to keep the garden looking good at all times.

One of the three island beds is planted only with evergreens — heathers, pines, and junipers. The large rock garden that runs along one side is planted with

◀ **Conifers for height** Mature cypresses at the back of the garden lift the view from the level plane. In winter the group is a dramatic focal point, with the golden conifer brightening up the grayest day.

Wood panel fencing

An aviary, housing tropical birds, is tucked behind the conifers.

The upright cypresses and golden conifers contrast in shape and color with rounded and narrow dwarf cultivars.

Two colorful island beds display shrubby fuchsias for spread and standard fuchsias for height and an edging of impatiens, salvias, and begonias.

Herbs, such as sage and thyme, grow among dwarf conifers, phlox, phormium, and irises.

Poles of sweet peas give height to the border.

A low wall edges the border and the lawn.

A central island bed holds pines, junipers, and heather.

A wooden bench faces a pleasant view across the garden.

A mixed border includes pansies, irises, and French marigolds, edged with mesembryanthemums.

Pyracantha, clematis, and ivy clamber up the wall above a raised container of fuchsias.

Shrubbery and trees frame a tiered rock garden.

An ornamental pool contains carp.

An immaculate lawn sets off the colorful borders and island beds.

An ivy-covered arch is a focal point above low-growing rock plants.

A large rock garden has mainly evergreen planting.

A specimen conifer hides a golden-leaved maple.

The patio, on stepped levels, is made of natural stone and precast stonelike concrete slabs.

A raised bed is planted with lobelias, calceolarias, alyssums, and geraniums.

A two-tier planting includes tuberous-rooted and wax begonias.

Urns and planters are filled with bedding plants — geraniums, helichrysums, alyssums, and lobelias.

A raised bed has a pink, blue, and white theme based on petunias, lobelias, and alyssums.

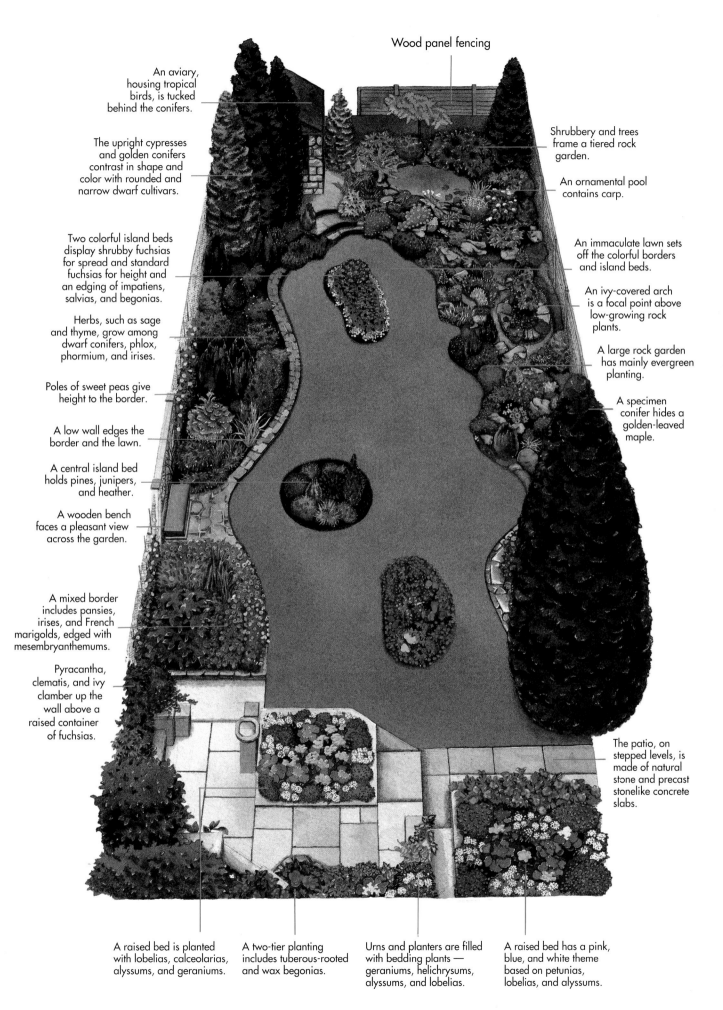

HOUSE

evergreen sempervivums and hebes, as well as several conifers in a range of foliage colors and shapes, varying from miniature and ground-hugging to columnar exclamation points for added height.

The use of tall, narrow conifers of various heights sets up a bold rhythm throughout the garden. Upright planting contrasts effectively with the more rounded forms of other conifers and low-growing shrubs, such as hebes and rock roses.

Different heathers, including winter-flowering types, act as year-round ground cover, visually weaving together the conifers. Evergreen rhododendrons offer colorful spring blooms. More spring flowers and fall color come from azaleas (*Rhododendron molle* cultivars). Maples provide height, brilliant fall color, and attractive bare winter branches.

◄ **Bedding plants** A frost-sensitive standard fuchsia rises above a froth of impatiens and tuberous begonias. The flowers of the green- and bronze-leaved wax begonias repeat the pink-and-red color theme.

THE ROCK GARDEN

The rock garden is planted with a mass of mainly evergreen species. The plan helps to identify the plants opposite.

1 Maiden pink (*Dianthus deltoides*)
2 Heather (*Calluna vulgaris*)
3 Hebe (*Hebe*)
4 Hens-and-chickens (*Sempervivum*)
5 Moss phlox (*Phlox subulata*)
6 Sun rose (*Helianthemum nummularium*)
7 *Fuchsia* 'Tom Thumb'
8 Bearberry (*Arctostaphylos uva-ursi*)
9 Dwarf juniper (*Juniperus communis* cultivars)
10 Japanese cedar (*Cryptomeria japonica*)
11 *Thujopsis dolabrata*
12 Dwarf blue spruce (*Picea pungens* cultivars)
13 Dwarf redwood (*Sequoia sempervirens* 'Adpressa')

14 Dwarf juniper (*Juniperus chinensis* cultivars)
15 Dwarf Lawson cypress (*Chamaecyparis lawsoniana* cultivars)
16 Stonecrop (*Sedum acre*)
17 Basket-of-gold (*Aurinia saxatilis*)
18 Knotweed (*Polygonum affine*)
19 Coralbells (*Heuchera sanguinea*)
20 Dwarf Hinoki cypress (*Chamaecyparis obtusa* cultivars)
21 Arborvitae (*Thuja occidentalis*)
22 *Rhododendron* hybrid
23 *Hydrangea macrophylla*
24 *Phlox paniculata*
25 Algerian ivy (*Hedera canariensis* 'Variegata')
26 Blue Atlas cedar (*Cedrus atlantica* 'Glauca')
27 Cucumber tree (*Magnolia acuminata*)
28 Purple-leaved cherry plum (*Prunus cerasifera* 'Atropurpurea')

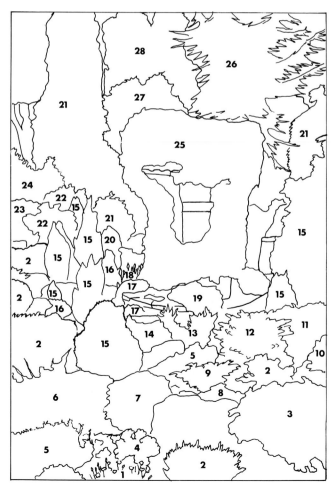

Snowdrops and crocuses give winter and early-spring interest. They are planted in pockets in the rock garden and come up year after year, gradually spreading to form wide clumps.

The lawn

The velvety lawn needs care and attention, but the result is worth the regular mowing, feeding, and edge trimming required. The neat carpet provides a restful contrast with the more colorful beds and borders. The stripes left by the mower echo the curves of flower beds and borders, as well as the shape of the garden.

Design features

The man-made, "hard" features in this garden comprise the patio, bench, decorative wall, ivy-covered arch, pool, rock garden, and aviary at the back. These have all been added over the years but were included in the original garden plan to avoid major alterations to established planting schemes.

The patio, as useful as it is ornamental, overlooks the whole of the garden. It is made of a mixture of stone materials.

At the far end of the garden is an aviary. In its place you could consider constructing a toolshed or a greenhouse. Alternatively, you could use the space to create a small vegetable patch.

▲ **Sunny retreat** A wooden bench on concrete supports is set between the two sweeping curves of the mixed border and looks across an island bed to the pool and rock garden beyond.

The wall behind ensures privacy and shelter, and the perforated concrete blocks and multicolored stonework add a decorative touch.

The island beds are set well inside the lawn to create mowing areas that are wider than the lawn mower. (Narrower strips of lawn are difficult to mow well, since the mower tends to scalp the turf as its wheels slip off the lawn edge and down into the adjacent bed.)

Equally practical is the low walling along the mixed border. It keeps the lawn truly separate from the border and prevents any grass from creeping out of one into the other.

▶ **Focal points** Near the patio is an ornamental pool, its still surface almost hidden in summer by the glossy floating leaves and brilliant blooms of hardy water lilies.

Designs for small gardens

A well-designed small garden minimizes the restrictions imposed by limited space and essentially becomes an extension of the house, an outdoor living room. A small garden is usually sheltered and can be turned into an inward-looking and secluded place for relaxation. Any disadvantages incurred by its size are outweighed by the corresponding ease with which it can be maintained.

Small gardens are often awkward in shape — long and narrow or squat and boxlike — but good design ideas can alter the perspective. Changes in level not only create walls down which plants can cascade, they can deceive the eye with the illusion of greater depth. Curving lines can do the same by leading the eye onward over a long, circuitous route rather than a short, straight one.

"Hard" landscape features — man-made furnishings — are especially important in small, enclosed gardens, where paving often replaces a conventional lawn and a formal pool or fountain may become the centerpiece of a courtyard.

Planting is limited in a small garden, so the choice of plants becomes even more important. The planting should be profuse enough to create a feeling of seclusion, yet avoid a cluttered look. Front gardens are often the most challenging to design, but even the smallest space has the potential to express its owner's personality.

A colorful embrace Astilbes, feverfew, and primroses reach out to greet this household's guests.

FIRST IMPRESSIONS

A fine front garden makes a fitting entrance to a home. Even the smallest lot has the potential to create a welcoming reception.

Whether it's for passersby, family, or guests, most people like their homes to look welcoming from the start and to reveal a bit of personal style. An attractive exterior is also an investment, enhancing a property's value.

Obviously, the larger the front yard, the greater the possibilities. But even if that space is minute, there is usually room for potted plants and greenery.

A tiny garden can hold surprisingly large plants. If there is room for only one or two shrubs, you may want to buy extra-large specimen plants for instant impact.

The soil in a small urban lot may be poor in nutrients and severely compacted. Liberal doses of compost, whether bought in bags or made at home, can work wonders of restoration.

Setting the tone

If possible, respond to the architectural style, mood, and scale of the house. A fine exterior, such as a well-proportioned Colonial or Federal facade, needs very little planting to emphasize its good points, while a house with little character might well benefit from an evergreen camouflage.

Plants and containers don't have to be historically accurate in relation to the house style, but they shouldn't look out of place.

Attention to detail is important, since a single window box or tub becomes an immediate focal point. Elaborately detailed planters are suitable for formal neoclassical

▼ **Warm welcome** A magnificent hortensia hydrangea by a bright red front door creates a cheerful impression. By fall the dead flower heads turn a nice russet-brown and continue to look attractive throughout the winter.

▲ **Climbing roses** Fragrant climbers of the repeat-flowering type provide a sweet-scented greeting of gorgeous blooms all summer. The yellow 'Casino' and the pink 'Compassion' have particularly heady scents. But roses need tying up, pruning, and deadheading, and in winter they can look gaunt. An evergreen honeysuckle could be planted as a companion for year-round cover and extra fragrance.

▶ **Front-door elegance** A single stone tub matches the classic simplicity of this front entrance. Planted with evergreen bay laurel and small-leaved ivy, it takes color in spring from daffodils and polyanthus primroses. The color scheme echoes that of the window box.

facades, wooden half barrels fit a cottage style, and simple terra-cotta pots go with anything. Containers with grand aspirations, such as stone urns, rarely look at ease in modest settings.

Most plants can be used formally or informally, but some plants set a particular style. Boxwood and bay laurel topiary conveys formality, while rampant honeysuckle does the opposite. This doesn't have to limit choice — cottage gardens traditionally offer a splendid mix of formal and informal plants.

Front doors and porches

Old-fashioned row houses and many modern urban condominiums have facades directly fronting the pavement, with one or more steps up to the front door.

Where space allows, a tub or a large flower pot is attractive. One good-size evergreen shrub — bay laurel, boxwood, fatsia, camellia, or aucuba — makes a better impression than many little plants. Bulbs and annuals can be added for seasonal interest and color.

A pair of tubs supporting the symmetry of a classical front door is impressive. If the entrance is narrow, vertically trained bay laurels or slim conifers are ideal.

Front-door tubs or pots for specimen plants should be at least 1 ft (30 cm) wide to look effective, retain moisture, and withstand a bump without toppling. If necessary, raise large containers on bricks for drainage.

Some houses have several steps up to the front door. If width allows, a row of flower pots can line one or both sides of the steps. Make sure they are stable, both for their safety and that of passersby. Large pots can be tucked in corners of the steps and house walls and climbers trained up and along any railings.

Climbers supported by a sturdy trellis or screw eyes and wires can be trained around a front door, open-fronted porch, or portico.

House walls

Before choosing a climbing plant for a house wall, decide just what effect you want to create. Some climbing plants, such as Virginia creeper, will cover an entire wall; others produce lovely flowers. Consider combining different plants — perhaps clematis and evergreen honeysuckle — to increase year-round visual interest.

▲ **Romantic dooryard** Flowers wash over a brick entryway to soften a harsh approach. In the foreground, the delicacy of hardy geraniums' rose-colored flowers contrasts with the opulence of a peony's blooms. *Clematis* 'Silver Moon' wreathes the house in flowers while annual nierembergias spill out of a pot.

▶ **Topiary sentinels** A fine exterior needs few decorative touches. Small-leaved boxwoods, clipped into spheres, emphasize this handsome front door. Such restrained elegance suits houses directly fronting the street.

Remember, many climbers need supports, and some climb rampantly. Pruning could well present problems if the house wall is high.

Be careful with self-clinging climbers, such as ivy, which can work their way into old mortar, causing it to flake or crumble. On painted walls the choice is limited to trellised plants that can be taken down during painting and then refastened in place.

Certain shrubs can be trained against a wall. Pyracantha and ceanothus are useful evergreen wall shrubs, and chaenomeles gives an early show of flowers.

Exposure is always important. Plants that will thrive by a south-facing wall may not grow well in

shade. Wall-trained plants benefit from the wall's shelter and latent warmth, allowing you to try types normally too cold sensitive for your region — a passionflower in southern zone 7, for example.

Window boxes, hanging baskets, and wall-hung half baskets can be fixed to a front facade. Wall-hung plants are most effective clustered near the door or window at eye level or just below, though a high hanging basket filled with trailing plants is enchanting. Make sure containers can be easily reached for watering.

Balconies range from window ledges with railings to generous walk-on decks. Plants can trail or grow upward to cover an area far greater than the balcony size. The higher a balcony is, the more exposed it may be, so delicate plants may be unsuitable.

Weight is an important factor, especially if the balcony is cantilevered. In such a situation, you should get the advice of a builder or an engineer before installing large containers. To lighten the load, use lightweight fiberglass or plastic containers and pot the plants into a peat-based mix in lieu of conventional potting soil.

If there is a basement area, consider planting a tall-growing climber, such as Boston ivy or wisteria, or a vigorous shrub, such as evergreen magnolia, for training up the front facade.

▲ **Old-world charm** A small cottage garden is a mass of summer colors from old-fashioned favorites — senecios, campanulas, roses, and potentillas. The focal point of the tiny, gravel-covered front garden is an urn filled with catmint (*Nepeta x faassenii*).

Minute gardens

As a rule, the smaller the garden, the simpler the layout should be. Attractive paving with a single pot-grown specimen shrub is often more appealing and sensible than a minuscule lawn. A gravel surface studded with clipped boxwood or bay laurel or with a multi-stemmed fig is also effective in a small lot.

▼ **Modern cottage garden** This alternative to the garden shown opposite is planted for interest throughout the year. Senecio furnishes masses of foliage until frost, while common jasmine by the house wall wafts fragrance through the air all summer. The colors are gentle, mainly greens and gold, with an emphasis on attractive leaf forms.

In one corner, behind a yellow-flowered crocosmia, is the soft green foliage of a white-flowered mock orange. The yellow spikes of *Verbascum* 'Gainsborough' contrast with *Rosa* 'Golden Wings.'

Foliage plants include golden marjoram, whose leaves remain yellow from spring until midsummer, as well as hostas and the felted silvery leaves of *Stachys byzantina.* Yellow Welsh poppies *(Meconopsis cambrica)* will self-seed in the garden.

Screening the boundary is *Pyracantha* 'Teton,' which bears yellow berries in fall. In front, the dwarf *Thuja occidentalis* 'Woodwardii' forms a dense globe of rich green.

In the foreground is a double row of shrubs. *Spiraea japonica* 'Gold Mound' fronts a golden-leaved evergreen berberis to make an informal low hedge.

Evergreens like *Juniperus communis depressa* 'Aurea' give a lovely glow. Also of value in winter is the summer-flowering *Hypericum* 'Hidcote,' which retains its leaves.

41

▲ Flowering hedges In spring forsythia bursts into glorious golden bloom, lasting for several weeks. It quickly forms a dense hedge from rooted cuttings planted 1 ft (30 cm) apart, and it responds well to clipping. Do not prune after early summer or you will cut off the flower buds for next year's display.

▶ Fragrant lavender Popular for path edging since the Middle Ages, lavender in shades of blue, pink, and pure white fills the air with its sweet scent on long summer days. Cut the faded flower stems back in late summer, and prune back hard in spring to keep the plants compact.

▲ **Roses all the way** A low picket fence supports the free-flowering climbing rose 'American Pillar' in New England style. On the house wall a vigorous rambling rose, the white 'Félicité et Perpétue,' adds to the rustic charm.

◄ **Town house style** This tiny front garden perfectly complements the house. It is contained within a low wall, stuccoed and painted to match the house walls, and is topped with decorative railings that add height without casting shade. A pair of standard roses and the white trellis also help to lift the view from ground level.

◀ **Front garden** Suburban gardens are often conventional in style, with a straight path, foundation plantings, and a specimen tree or shrub. The choice of plants, however, can transform an ordinary garden into an outstanding one.

Here, two focal points near the property line immediately attract the eye. By the house is a smoke tree *(Cotinus coggygria)*, whose feathery, hazy purple flower clusters in summer are followed by brilliant leaf colors in fall. Near the front hedge of golden privet is a purple-leaved cherry plum *(Prunus cerasifera* 'Atropurpurea'), which is a mass of blooms in spring.

A white climbing rose, 'Iceberg,' and an ornamental vine with rich fall tints embellish the walls.

▶ **Town garden** The brick edging around the flagstone terrace blends well with the house, and strong plant shapes make a memorable first impression.

The symmetrical design is accentuated with a low lavender hedge and with stone urns containing dwarf chamaecyparises. Year-round color comes from other evergreens — mahonias, Portuguese laurel, clipped senecios in beds by the windows, and a neat boxwood hedge behind ornamental railings.

The house wall is draped with wisteria, but what really catches the eye is a magnificent evergreen *Magnolia grandiflora*.

◀ **Open-plan garden** Sometimes, front yards flow one into another without divisions to mark property lines. Here, individual character has been emphasized without destroying the air of openness.

Irregularly shaped beds set into the lawn are planted with ground-hugging shrubs and perennials, including hostas, lady's-mantle, and bergenias — all with attractive leaves.

The specimen tree is a weeping willow-leaved pear *(Pyrus salicifolia)*. Clipped bay laurels flank the door, and a pyracantha is trained against the house wall. A curving path helps to disguise the linear outline of the lot.

LONG AND NARROW PLOTS

Creative design ideas can release a garden from a regimented appearance and turn it into a pleasant outdoor living room for the family.

The majority of gardens are created along straight lines, which can work well on the average property. But when the yard is long and narrow, this approach emphasizes the constriction of the space. Here, it is better to abandon this linear design style and follow curving lines and introduce judiciously placed focal points to leave the onlooker with an impression of greater breadth.

Traditionally, a path leads from the house to the back of the garden. In long gardens, this has the effect of cutting the plot into two narrow strips, which create an even greater feeling of claustrophobia. A path need not lead straight down the middle of the yard but should curve along one side to make the garden look wider. Giving flowing rather than straight edges to the lawn produces the same effect. Varying the width of the lawn also varies the depth of the borders, which makes it possible to create more interesting planting schemes.

Garden divisions

Long, narrow gardens, such as the one featured here, are a challenge. The object is to soften and conceal the narrow proportions. Here, this has been achieved by dividing the garden into a series of simple areas, each leading into the next in a smoothly flowing design and each stretching across the yard's width. Within the garden's divisions, there's plenty of scope to include elements that meet the whole family's needs.

The garden has three divisions: the two-level patio, a lawn, and an area paved with stone, which is accessed via a pergola. The wide, shrub-filled borders on either side of the pergola create a

narrow entranceway and, because they partially obscure the back of the garden, add an element of mystery. You can imagine the garden extending well beyond its actual boundary.

A family garden

The divisions in this garden are both practical and attractive, suiting children and adults alike. There is a swing for the children

and, more important, a good-size lawn and patio on which to play. All of the areas in this yard are child-resistant. Fragile plantings, however beautiful, would only become a source of friction in a family garden.

Adults find the patio and lawn equally pleasurable, both to look at and to use. The patio is ideal for entertaining, whether for a large-scale barbecue, coffee with

---

▶ **Visual deception** The long, narrow outline of this garden has disappeared. The new design has introduced curves along the perimeter and changes in level near the house, creating separate areas for different activities yet maintaining unity and harmony.

▲ Patio and steps This bird's-eye view shows the two-level patio and wide, shallow steps with large groups of container plants.

the neighbors, or just sitting outdoors. Although the garden faces north, the house is low enough so that the sun can reach most areas for most of the day in summer. The barbecue and table are near the house, and the barbecue is portable for easy storage.

The flower beds also contain a range of vegetables, such as scarlet runner beans, mingling with the flowers, as well as plenty of shrubs for winter interest. A few well-placed trees add height but are not so high that they overshadow the garden.

A path of hexagonal pavers curves gently, leading the eye (as well as the feet) to the white pergola, which half conceals the small greenhouse behind. Finishing touches include low raised planting beds and numerous container plantings, which provide splashes of color.

Level changes

A garden with level changes is visually more attractive than one on a flat plane. It gives an impression of enclosure, shelter, and privacy in the low-lying area and a sense of opening out where the level rises. This low-level patio takes on the feeling of a room — but very much a room with a view. The house walls shield the patio further, while the generously wide steps beckon the eye to admire the garden beyond.

The steps connect the upper and

▼ Barbecue area Safely away from general garden traffic, the barbecue becomes a center of activity in summer. Plants in pots and planting pockets enliven the area without turning the steps into an obstacle course.

lower garden levels. In addition, they provide informal seating for children, who rarely use chairs if given a chance to sit elsewhere. The steps also provide space for setting out seasonal displays of flowers in pots.

The plants-in-pots theme is repeated on the patio itself and, Mediterranean style, in a flat-backed container hung on the wall high enough above the barbecue not to be singed. Hard surfaces, whether horizontal or vertical, make an excellent setting for plants, and both benefit visually. The natural beauty and irregular growth of the plants soften the harsh materials and hard geometry; the plain background of masonry and concrete shows up and enhances individual plants in a way that is rarely possible in beds or borders.

The patio is paved in concrete slabs colored and molded to look like squares of granite blocks. Two geometric patterns — blocks in straight rows and quarter circles — are laid imaginatively to create a semiabstract pattern. Another approach would be to lay a series of four quarter-circle slabs together to create several large circular patterns. Other options using concrete include slabs colored and textured to look either like flagstones or rows of

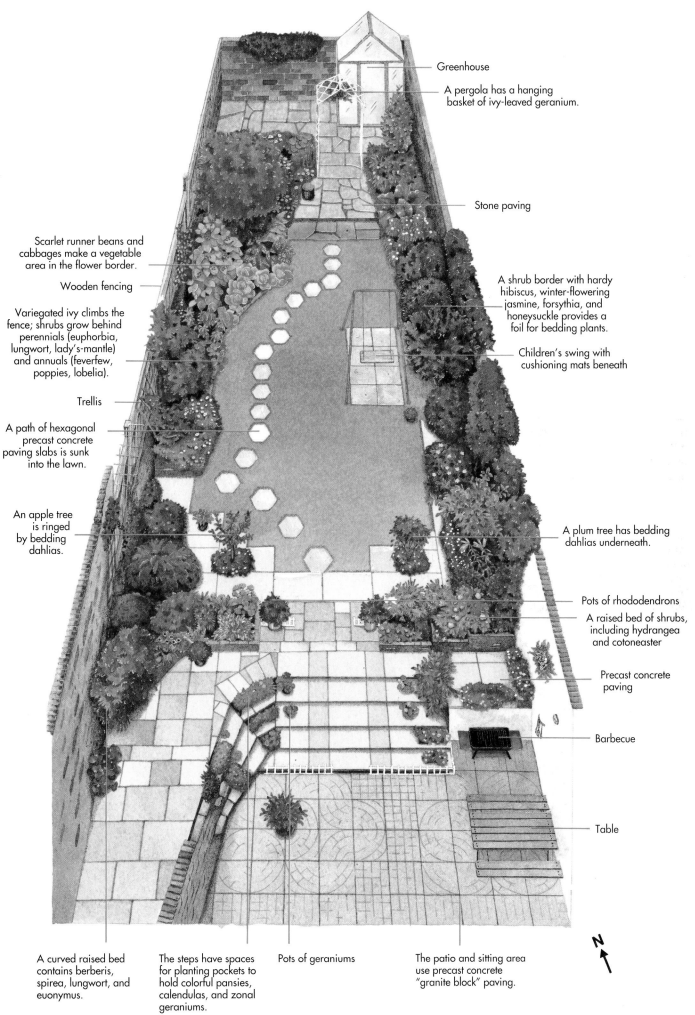

Greenhouse

A pergola has a hanging basket of ivy-leaved geranium.

Stone paving

A shrub border with hardy hibiscus, winter-flowering jasmine, forsythia, and honeysuckle provides a foil for bedding plants.

Children's swing with cushioning mats beneath

A plum tree has bedding dahlias underneath.

Pots of rhododendrons

A raised bed of shrubs, including hydrangea and cotoneaster

Precast concrete paving

Barbecue

Table

Scarlet runner beans and cabbages make a vegetable area in the flower border.

Wooden fencing

Variegated ivy climbs the fence; shrubs grow behind perennials (euphorbia, lungwort, lady's-mantle) and annuals (feverfew, poppies, lobelia).

Trellis

A path of hexagonal precast concrete paving slabs is sunk into the lawn.

An apple tree is ringed by bedding dahlias.

A curved raised bed contains berberis, spirea, lungwort, and euonymus.

The steps have spaces for planting pockets to hold colorful pansies, calendulas, and zonal geraniums.

Pots of geraniums

The patio and sitting area use precast concrete "granite block" paving.

N

HOUSE

bricks. Alternatively, you could use the actual material.

The steps and upper garden immediately surrounding the patio are paved in concrete slabs of varied size and color. The paving and the lawn interlock in a staggered pattern — a more unusual approach than a straight line.

Another contrast of "soft" and "hard" landscape is the series of planting pockets created by leaving gaps in the paving at the edges of the steps (where they won't trip pedestrians). Eliminating the corner reduces the need to custom-cut paving slabs and softens a hard edge.

The raised flower beds on the upper patio create a third level change. Shrubs and colorful annuals spill over the low brick walls, becoming a gateway of greenery into the garden beyond. The gateway idea is repeated in the miniature fencing that runs across the foot of the steps and the patio's entrance to the lawn.

An alternative design

An alternative plan (see page 50) for this property used similar elements — lawn, patio, barbecue, greenhouse, flowers, shrubs, fruit trees, vegetables, and children's play area — but assembled them in a simpler design. Here, internal spaces echo the garden's rectilinear outline, but by dividing the area into compartments they

▲ **Spotted lungwort** Also known as Bethlehem sage, *Pulmonaria saccharata* relishes the shade. Its large silver-marbled leaves provide year-round ground cover. The bed is enlivened in spring with pink and blue flower clusters and later with the bright yellow of annual calendulas *(Calendula officinalis)* and the lime-green feathery sprays of *Alchemilla mollis.*

▶ **Curving path** Hexagonal precast paving slabs are set just below the lawn level for easy mowing. The line follows the curved edge of the border from the upper patio, with its planting pockets and raised beds, to the paved service area and greenhouse at the end of the garden.

make the garden appear shorter and wider.

The paving contrasts brick with plain concrete slabs. One large planting bed marks the transition from the patio area to the garden beyond. The uncluttered rectangular lawn extends from the wall to the path, which runs along a narrow border. A clipped yew hedge hides the vegetable garden and service area with the greenhouse from general view.

The garden is easy to maintain, with plenty of scope for recreation and relaxation.

A sandbox is situated within sight of the house and patio. At a later stage, it can easily be converted into an ornamental pool or a miniature rock garden.

◄ **Mixed border** Vegetable plants are grown among ornamentals in the wide, curving border. Other tall-growing plants include late-summer-flowering hybrid goldenrods (*Solidago* cultivars), with spotted lungwort and nasturtiums spilling over the edge.

▼ **Raised bed** Close to the patio, a raised bed planted with tall-growing shrubs and climbers ensures privacy from the neighboring house. A honeysuckle (*Lonicera japonica*) trained along the fence adds fragrance above clumps of lilies. White achilleas and yellow loosestrife (*Lysimachia punctata*) contrast well with pots of rich blue trailing lobelia.

▶ **Pergolas**
These come in a range of styles and materials to suit all types of gardens. Painted wooden pergolas, like the one on the right, need regular maintenance.

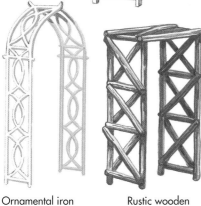

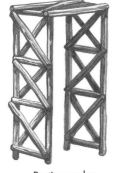

Ornamental iron

Rustic wooden

ALTERNATIVE DESIGN

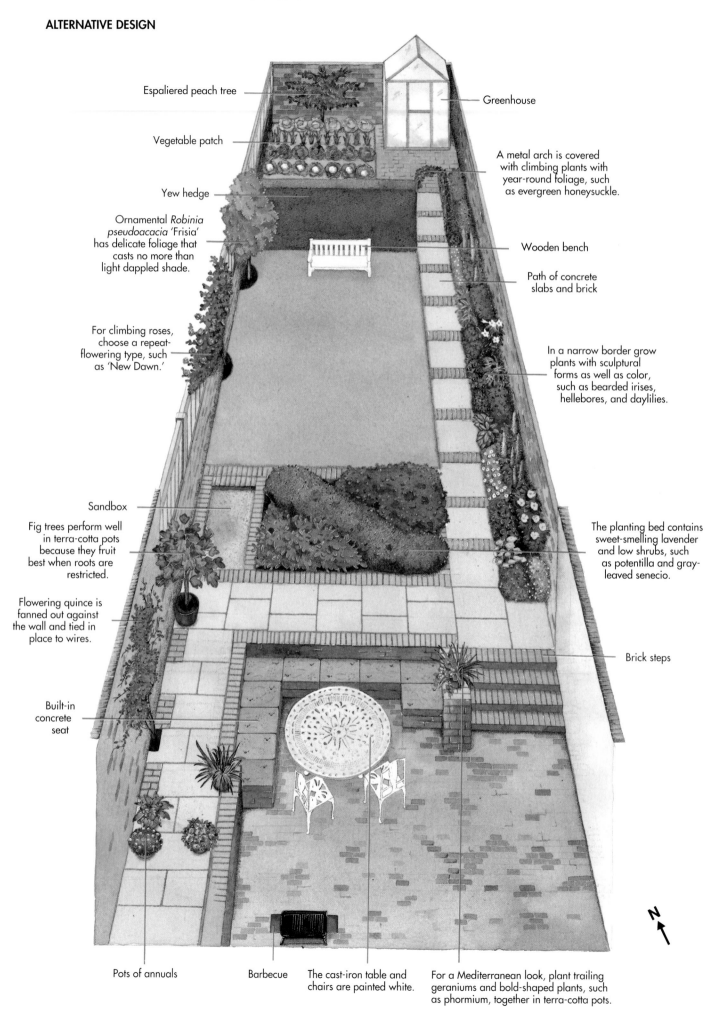

Espaliered peach tree

Greenhouse

Vegetable patch

A metal arch is covered with climbing plants with year-round foliage, such as evergreen honeysuckle.

Yew hedge

Ornamental *Robinia pseudoacacia* 'Frisia' has delicate foliage that casts no more than light dappled shade.

Wooden bench

Path of concrete slabs and brick

For climbing roses, choose a repeat-flowering type, such as 'New Dawn.'

In a narrow border grow plants with sculptural forms as well as color, such as bearded irises, hellebores, and daylilies.

Sandbox

Fig trees perform well in terra-cotta pots because they fruit best when roots are restricted.

The planting bed contains sweet-smelling lavender and low shrubs, such as potentilla and gray-leaved senecio.

Flowering quince is fanned out against the wall and tied in place to wires.

Brick steps

Built-in concrete seat

Pots of annuals

Barbecue

The cast-iron table and chairs are painted white.

For a Mediterranean look, plant trailing geraniums and bold-shaped plants, such as phormium, together in terra-cotta pots.

HOUSE

N

USING RIGHT ANGLES

**A simple, crisp design and inspired planting
have helped to transform a small rectangular lot
into an elegant garden.**

When faced with a rectangular lot, the first instinct of many gardeners is to counteract the right angles with curves: curved paths, lawns, beds, borders, and even circular ornamental pools.

This is often attractive, but a garden that turns the limitations of a rectangular layout into a positive design element can also be appealing. A garden that emphasizes its right-angled geometry can be very crisp and refreshing.

The key here is to implement a simple design, using a clean, bold layout and good-quality but plain furnishings and paving materials. To soften straight lines, install dense informal planting.

Though this garden has the benefit of mature trees and shrubs, hard, sharp edges in a new garden can be effectively softened with quick-growing annuals, climbers, and perennials until the slower-growing woody plants begin to make an impact.

The site and layout

This rectangular, level garden is in a middle-class urban neighborhood. A large paved area extends from the house roughly to the middle of the backyard and is surrounded on three sides by a low stone retaining wall. Behind the wall are raised planting beds and a large raised L-shaped pool, the garden's main attraction.

The overall effect is one of

▼ **Spring color** Lily-flowered tulips — 'China Pink,' yellow 'West Point,' and 'White Triumphator' — seem all the more spectacular when viewed against a backdrop of foliage and reflected in the still water of the pool.

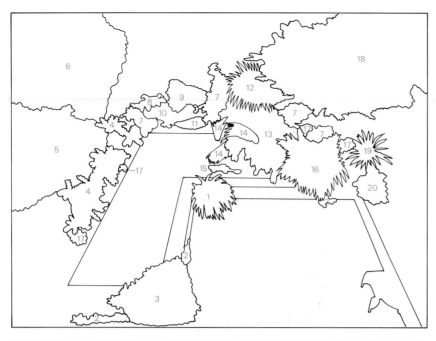

SUMMER SCENE

Boundary greenery — some "borrowed" from neighboring gardens — forms a backdrop to enclose this elegant urban garden. The plan shown above identifies the main plants on the right.

1 Kaffir lily *(Clivia miniata)*
2 English ivy *(Hedera helix)*
3 Oregon grape *(Nematanthus)*
4 *Mahonia nervosa*
5 California privet *(Ligustrum ovalifolium)*
6 *Magnolia grandiflora*
7 *Ligularia dentata*
8 *Hosta 'Royal Standard'*

9 Dwarf bamboo *(Pleioblastus humilis)*
10 Lady fern *(Athyrium filix-femina)*
11 Sweet woodruff *(Galium odoratum)*
12 Feather grass *(Stipa gigantea)*
13 Arrowhead *(Sagittaria)*
14 Cattail *(Typha minima)*
15 Miniature water lily *(Nymphaea hybrid)*
16 Fountain grass *(Pennisetum orientale)*
17 *Impatiens wallerana*
18 Chinese privet *(Ligustrum lucidum)*
19 Spanish dagger *(Yucca gloriosa)*
20 Chinese hibiscus *(Hibiscus rosa-sinensis)*

pleasant enclosure, reinforced by tall perimeter planting beyond. Access from the house is through French doors, which are flanked by tall, vertical glass panels and topped by a huge, semicircular window — an impressive feature visible from the garden.

Surrounded by mature landscapes on all sides, this garden benefits from neighbors' plantings — most notably a magnificent mature evergreen magnolia growing next door but overhanging the pool.

Other tall shrubs and trees in adjacent yards help to create a sense of high-level enclosure, which is kept comfortably open at ground level by the broad expanse of paving and water. The neighboring shrubs and trees also blur the garden's boundaries, making the plot seem larger than it actually is.

Masonry

The masonry here is attractive and unpretentious. Large rectangular slate paving slabs are laid in straight rows, with tightly butted open joints and staggered cross joints.

Minor variations in tone, from cool to rosy grays, and natural variations in surface texture create quiet, subtle patterns.

The raised pool wall continues the theme of natural stone, its irregularly shaped stones contrasting in scale and texture with the larger slate slabs. The wall varies in construction from tight, parallel courses to a more random effect, rather like a vertical jigsaw puzzle.

The flat stone coping on top of the pool wall emphasizes the formal geometry, and its pale tone makes the water seem darker and more mysterious. The coping provides extra seating and a vantage point from which to view the goldfish.

An old brick wall bounds one side of the garden; vertical fencing of close-set wooden boards encloses the rest of the area. Over time, both have weathered to soft tones, the silvery gray wood offering a variation on the gray of the paving.

General planting

The planting is mixed in the best sense of the word: bright splashes of seasonal color provided by popular, easily available plants — bulbs, for example — positioned against a background of permanent trees and shrubs, including a good proportion of evergreens for winter cover.

Though not a purely foliage garden — flowers are included, and many of the plants have unmemorable leaves — there is enough outstanding foliage to make an overall impact. Variegated and nongreen leaves are deliberately excluded to provide a restful background for bursts of color from the flowers.

Variation, instead, comes from scale and form: enormous round leaves, lacy fronds, and grassy upright or arching foliage, itself providing contrast with the bold horizontal planes of the paving and water.

A large multistemmed Chinese privet punctuates one end of the pool, and large hollies create a dense screen at the back of the garden. In a long, narrow planting bed next to the pool, a row of

◀ **Focal point** The L-shaped pool is the dominant feature in this small garden. It is framed by pleasing greenery from mature trees and shrubs that give a sense of secluded enclosure. Around the pool grow such moisture lovers as hostas, ferns, and bamboos above a ground cover of sweet woodruff. The pool itself is stocked with cattails, large-leaved arrowheads, and water lilies (with their roots confined in submerged tubs).

▼ **Fountains and water** From a raised bed, a huge mound of Oriental fountain grass *(Pennisetum orientale)* arches its foliage and soft catkinlike seed heads over the pool edge. It breaks up the severe lines of the coping and contrasts in form and texture with a nearby spiky yucca.

evergreen mahonias creates a solid barrier, with whorls of leaves at slightly different heights and angles setting up a pleasing rhythm.

Where the raised beds widen, there are bay laurels and kalmias as well as evergreen honeysuckle *(Lonicera fragrantissima)*. Ivy is used as a climber and for ground cover, even gaining a foothold in the narrow joints between the paving and the wall.

Red and yellow flowers predominate; grouped in large masses, they are surrounded by dense greenery. Along with red, yellow, pink, and white tulips — all planted in broad beds of single colors — there are daffodils and forget-me-nots for an early show.

By the time the spring display finishes and bulbs are lifted or die back, herbaceous perennials have taken over, covering the ground and giving new color.

SECLUDED GARDENS

**Many gardens lack privacy, but with an
imaginative design and bold planting, a garden
can become a haven of tranquillity.**

Seclusion is an important element in most gardens, and there are several ways of creating your own private haven. The garden featured on these pages is very well planned, with excellent design qualities that provide several good ideas to help you achieve this kind of intimacy.

Brick walls act as a good sound barrier by minimizing noise from traffic and neighbors. They also effectively hide any eyesores beyond and define the extent of the garden space.

An important point to remember is not to build walls or fences too high, because this can create a feeling of claustrophobia. This problem has been successfully overcome here by the introduction of a purely ornamental archway, blocked by a wrought-iron gate.

Besides alleviating any feelings of being hemmed in, the gate (which doesn't open) lets you look at the vista outside and makes the garden seem larger.

Hedges, although not as effective as masonry in reducing noise, do provide an alternative way of preserving the privacy of a garden, especially if they are evergreen, dense, and tall. Closely planted firethorn *(Pyracantha)*, cherry laurel *(Prunus laurocerasus)*, and Japanese yew *(Taxus cuspidata)* are suitable hedge plants.

Plants and masonry

An economical option that successfully breaks up the monotony of a brick wall is to leave gaps within the brickwork for planting. You can also decorate the top of the wall with plants.

Another choice, which has been used here, is to add a trellis above the wall. This acts as a decorative screen and can be covered within a year or two by such rampant climbers as *Clematis armandii*, crimson glory vine *(Vitis coignetiae)*, Boston ivy *(Parthenocissus tricuspidata)*, hederas, or the white-flowered climbing hydrangea *(Hydrangea petiolaris)*.

Vertical gardening

A newly erected brick wall can, at first, appear rather harsh. It is a good idea to use climbing plants to soften this effect. There is an

▼ **Background trees** Mature trees, in the garden and beyond, define the boundaries and enclose this private garden in a vibrant tapestry of green and golden colors.

The lawn is a relaxing and sheltered open space.

The cast-iron permanent outdoor furniture is painted white.

This *Robinia* echoes one on the other side of the gate and lights up the rear of the garden.

A wrought-iron gate offers views outside the garden.

The golden green leaves of *Robinia pseudoacacia* 'Frisia' provide color and seclusion.

Brick steps link the garden proper with the sunken patio.

Evergreen shade-loving plants — ferns, mahonia, and *Fatsia japonica* — thrive in the dappled shade of the *Robinia*.

Bold hosta foliage creates good visual contrast with the swordlike leaves of the yucca.

An edging of annual ageratums forms a dominant splash of bluish pink in summer.

The legs of an old treadle sewing machine are used for a table that matches the overall garden style.

N

HOUSE

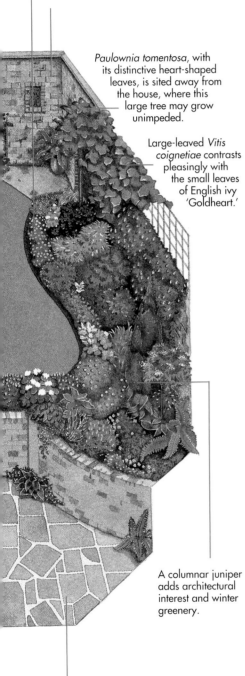

Annuals, like these marigolds, are planted in bold swaths to avoid a cluttered look.

Niched brick walls form a decorative corner feature.

Paulownia tomentosa, with its distinctive heart-shaped leaves, is sited away from the house, where this large tree may grow unimpeded.

Large-leaved *Vitis coignetiae* contrasts pleasingly with the small leaves of English ivy 'Goldheart.'

A columnar juniper adds architectural interest and winter greenery.

Stone paving covers the patio area in an irregular but well-laid-out pattern.

abundance of flowering climbers and a variety of ivies that will readily and rapidly grow up walls facing in any direction and enhance the whole garden.

English ivy *(Hedera helix)* grows so abundantly that the newness of any brick wall can be obliterated within a year. Bear in mind, though, that if a few gaps in the covering expose the brickwork, it is more appealing than a solid green blanket. The lush foliage setting of this garden is achieved by contrasting hues of green — for example, the light-colored leaves of the golden locust *(Robinia pseudoacacia* 'Frisia') set against the darker ivy-clad perimeter walls of the garden.

Patio and steps

The stone paving of the patio area is laid in a pattern of large and small paving slabs embedded in cement. It extends across the width of the site, with access from the house through French doors. The patio is on a lower level than the garden itself, but the two are linked with a flight of brick steps, whose curving line is echoed in the abutting wall.

The patio is a place for relaxing and is large enough for informal entertaining. The planting is contained within brick-edged beds, containers, and pockets along the base of the low walls. Sheltered on all sides, the patio receives afternoon and evening sun.

The steps are comfortably shallow and wide, leading, via a stone-paved path, to the gate, thus helping to create an illusion of space.

The furniture is a positive feature in its own right and part of the overall master design. The wrought-iron table and bench are matched by the slender banister alongside the steps and ornate chairs on the lawn. They are all painted white for maximum impact. The subtle and rather ornamental wrought-iron gate, fitted into the brickwork archway, completes the theme.

In a small, well-planned garden, weatherproof outdoor furniture is an advantage, though it does need regular maintenance to look its best. Folding tables and chairs must be stored inside when not in use, which is an inconvenience. The furniture shown here is expensive but, as a garden ornament in its own right, gives the garden a more inviting look.

▼ **Shelter and seclusion** Safe from prying eyes and disturbing traffic noises, this little oasis looks across bright bedding plants and a velvety lawn to a soothing forest of foliage.

◀ **Peaceful greens** The patio is surrounded by foliage plants carefully chosen for their contrasts in color and form — the huge hand-shaped and leathery leaves of *Fatsia japonica* beneath the finely divided golden green leaf sprays of a locust (*Robinia pseudoacacia* 'Frisia'). Below and opposite this tree are the spiky, white-edged leaves of a container-grown yucca, backed up by blue-green hosta foliage and bright green arching fern fronds.

Pots and baskets of wax begonias punctuate the greenery with bright splashes of summer color.

▼ **Garden statues** Inanimate objects can be difficult to site successfully, but the statue within the curved brick wall at the patio's end looks perfect — the ideal focal point for the sea of bedding and foliage plants at its foot. In the background a bust nearly fills a niche in the ivy-covered boundary wall.

Plants in pots and urns provide an additional level of planting, which punctuates and accentuates the overall design. Flower-filled containers add splashes of color. These are tempered by the cooler hues and strong forms of the containers filled with hostas and yuccas.

Lawn centerpiece

The two main features in this garden, the patio and the lawn, are shut off from the outside world by brick walls and mature trees. From the patio, the lawn appears larger than it actually is, partly because of its uncluttered expanse and partly because of its curving lines, which flow easily into the mixed borders along the garden boundaries.

With its complete privacy, the lawn is perfect for sunbathing. It has a soothing and restful effect, wonderful in the evening, when the trees and shrubs cast their lengthening shadows. The smooth green expanse holds together the wide borders that are filled with shrubs, herbaceous perennials, and colorful bedding plants.

Such fine turf is achieved only through loving care. Frequent mowing and edging, regular feeding, and watering are the essential and, unfortunately, monotonous tasks that a gardener must be prepared to undertake in the pursuit of a perfect lawn.

Focal points

Throughout the garden are hidden little secrets, important for their individual impact yet blending naturally into the design. Carefully chosen statues that reflect the owners' personal style

◀ **Shade lovers** In dappled shade for part of the day, the raised beds by the patio are filled with plants that thrive in just such conditions. Ferns and the tall, handsome leafy stems of Solomon's seal (Polygonatum x hybridum) arch over a footing of annual impatiens. The colorful carpet is broken by a small-leaved trailing ivy.

▼ **Wall ornaments** The far corner of the garden, a spot easy to ignore, is a design feature of restrained elegance here. The brick wall is pierced with a small niche containing a stone bust, and farther along it is adorned with decorative tiles, set flush in the walls like windows, and terra-cotta plaques. The crowning touch is a huge urn containing a handsome specimen of the male fern (Dryopteris filix-mas). It contrasts well with the bold foliage of the nearby empress tree (Paulownia tomentosa).

and taste are strategically placed in the greenery — an inscrutable greyhound gazing across the patio, a neoclassical bust in a wall niche, and a graceful figurine rising like the mythical Aphrodite from a sea of impatiens. These garden statues lend substance to clumps of shade-loving ferns and hostas and break up the solidity of the walls. A terra-cotta urn positioned in the far corner draws the eye from the patio along a diagonal line that visually distorts and extends the distance.

A garden for dreams

The peacefulness and seclusion of this garden has been achieved, at some expense, through a combination of clever design and architecture and through bold planting ideas. Like any other mature garden, it has been years in the making, and the years to come will mellow any harshness of the surrounding walls and the stone paving.

The garden is by no means low maintenance — bedding plants must be renewed according to the changing seasons, climbers must be pruned to keep them within bounds, and container plantings need regular watering and feeding throughout the growing season.

The result, though, is a green and restful sanctuary, a place in which to dream the dream of all gardeners — the creation of their ideal garden.

COURTYARD GARDENS

Small urban gardens are often enclosed by high walls and neighboring trees. A creative design can turn these into positive features.

City gardens typically suffer from shade, poor and dry soil, lack of privacy, and lack of space — problems that many yards in heavily developed suburban areas share. Luckily, you can create privacy and an illusion of light and improve the soil. Besides, with a small yard you can lavish far more dollars per square foot without breaking your budget, and you can give more attention to details than with large gardens.

Shade cast by nearby buildings is unalterable, but shade from overhanging trees can be lessened by thinning the branches. Often neighbors will even let you prune their trees, if you pay an arborist to do the job. Beware, though, of cutting down large trees — it may benefit the plants underneath but harm the overall landscape.

Try painting walls white to reflect additional light onto nearby plants and give an illusion of space. Pale foliage and pastel flowers also enhance the sense of brightness.

Improving the soil

The soil found in city backyards, and indeed on most new construction sites, is typically poor in structure and nutrients, resulting in disappointing plant growth. It can be improved by working in bulky organic matter. Compost or manure sold in bags by garden centers is good for this purpose.

▼ **False perspective** This long and narrow courtyard garden has been given a sense of space and depth by an avenue of terracotta pots leading the eye toward a group of slender Italianate cypresses at the garden's end.

Topsoil can be bought in bulk but is expensive, and quality varies. An annual mulch of shredded bark or wood chips increases a soil's moisture retention and is a good soil conditioner. Regular feeds with quick-acting fertilizer provide nutrients immediately.

Good-quality loam-based potting soil gives container plantings a head start, and there are special peat-enriched mixes for camellias, rhododendrons, and other acid-loving plants.

Creating privacy
Old brick walls can look beautiful, and new ones mellow relatively quickly, giving a cozy enclosed feeling — but the cost of materials and labor is very high. Thin walls of trellises or wooden fence panels can create privacy more cheaply.

Covered with deciduous climbers, a trellis lets in the maximum amount of light during winter yet filters light in summer, when a garden is used most. Compact deciduous trees trained as standards, with the branches pruned up above head height, also work well seasonally and save space.

Urban planting
Plant growth in urban conditions or on any type of confined site with compacted, poor-quality soil is often slow. Large plants have instant impact and, though expensive, can prove to be a sensible investment. However, they take longer to become established than small ones and need lots of water.

Planting closer together than normal is also justified in such a small garden; again, this requires extra feeding and watering. In addition, be prepared to thin the planting later on.

City gardens are often too shady for a good lawn or too small to make grass cutting worthwhile. Choose a form of attractive paving instead.

◀ **Foliage dressing** Glowing red brick laid in a traditional basket-weave pattern makes an excellent contrast for the dark green wall coverings of Boston ivy and ornamental vines. At ground level brick-red pots of clipped boxwood echo the color scheme.

▶ **Centerpoint** A circular pool surmounted by an ornamental birdbath introduces a different geometric shape to counteract the straight lines elsewhere in the garden. A wreath of small-leaved ivy, which responds well to clipping, surrounds the base of the pool, which is guarded by two ornamental cranes poised to catch the goldfish in the pool.

▼ **Flights of fancy** Wide brick steps leading out to the garden are marked with bold terra-cotta finials set on plinths. A low, densely clipped boxwood hedge and standard-trained gardenias repeat the architectural design of the courtyard garden below.

A good proportion of evergreens gives small gardens an interesting look year-round.

Formal brick

Where space is precious, lots are often irregular and there may not be room to hide the shape. In the example shown here, the gardener has taken good advantage of an L-shaped backyard by turning the long, narrow leg of the "L" into a plant-filled corridor and the square base near the house into a peaceful retreat.

Here, restraint is the dominant theme: the color scheme is based on variations of brick-red, terracotta, and dark green, and though some plants blossom, they do so incidentally.

The layout is largely symmetrical — the few exceptions are due to the garden's basic shape or to whim. The stately steps, with their mirror-image ball finials, clipped hedges, and topiary trees, align with the long corridor.

The fountain is central to the square, but asymmetrical when viewed from the house, making a pleasing break from static formality. And a sitting area with a low wooden table is tucked into a corner that affords both shelter and privacy from onlookers behind the glass doors.

Masonry
Restricting the number of materials used creates a feeling of space in a small garden. Surfaces appear to flow into one another, disguising the real dimensions. Here, close-butted brick paving and low walls repeat the brick theme of the house and existing garden walls.

The brick paving is laid in a traditional, unobtrusive basket-weave pattern. On a practical level, using small units such as brick (as opposed to large flagstones, for example) allows the paving to adjust to uneven foundations and possible subsidence without ugly cracking. Such a pavement can also easily incorporate preexisting features, such as drains.

Bricks — laid flat for risers and on edge for treads — form the steps that connect the small upper entranceway to the lower level of the garden. Brick edging to the beds reinforces the geometry and, on a practical note, prevents soil from spilling onto the paving.

Formal planting
Restraint and architectural form prevail, with dark green topiary and dark green climbers that take the shapes of the walls they cover. Boxwood is clipped into either right-angled hedges, repeating the lines of the house and layout, or topiary balls, echoing the shape of the finials. The round base of the fountain is surrounded by an immaculate ivy ring and filled with water lilies.

In the corridor is a "forest" of clipped boxwood balls, shortest in front and tallest behind. This gives a sense of depth and space to the corridor, as does a group of tall, columnar cypresses at the far end of the garden.

Temporary summer features, which must be protected from frost during the winter months, include huge pots of cycads, or sago palms *(Cycas revoluta)*, maidenhair fern, and standard-trained gardenias. The cycads, with their concentric rosettes, and the ferns, with their arching, fountainlike fronds, heighten the air of formality. The clipped gardenias repeat the shape of the topiary boxwood balls. In contrast, sprawling mint is contained within a terra-cotta pot, preventing its roots from spreading rapidly throughout the garden.

Several self-clinging climbers cover the walls: trumpet creeper, ornamental grape, Boston ivy, English ivy, and Chinese jasmine *(Trachelospermum jasminoides)*. The star jasmine provides a summer display of scented white flowers, followed by the scarlet trumpets of *Campsis radicans*. The deciduous Boston ivy *(Parthenocissus tricuspidata)* bears a modest number of blue-black berries, and its leaves turn orange and scarlet.

Features and focal points
The central feature is a two-tier round stone basin, with a pineapple fountain head and goldfish in the lower pool. Two antique-style Chinese cranes watch over the fish, discouraging real birds from poaching them.

▶**Soothing touches** The steps in this small urban garden have been given a new look with treads of concrete slabs. They will mellow with time; meanwhile their bright appearance is softened by an evergreen mahonia, colorful tulips, and a flowering crab apple tree.

SUNKEN GARDENS

**Given an attractive layout and suitable plants,
a small, low-lying garden can be turned into a stunningly
beautiful spot and a restful retreat.**

Town houses that were built when coal was used for heat often have a sunken utility area at either the front or the back, through which coal was chuted down to an indoor bin. Modern houses set into the side of a hill may have something similar — though the purpose is drainage. In either case a sunken area in a tiny yard can be depressing. But with imaginative design, you can transform such a confined space into a leafy retreat.

In fact, a sunken area offers a warm, sheltered microclimate. And because this type of garden is usually small, it is easier to afford top-quality materials, such as stone, brick, or trellising.

The site
This garden, attached to a Victorian row house, is rectangular, with a long, narrow extension 4 ft (1.2 m) below the main area, creating an L shape. It is surrounded by high brick walls, which have been made

even taller by the addition of trellises at the top.

The garden plan makes the most of the feeling of space and luxuriant greenery, while achieving privacy by excluding unpleasant sights outside and at the same time screening neighbors' views into the garden.

This is a high-maintenance garden, but is attractive in every season. There is a continuous floral display from midspring until the first fall frosts.

The design
To provide privacy and help camouflage the small size of the garden, the boundary walls have been raised, then hidden with dense planting. The extra height provides more space for vertical gardening and increases the number of climbers and wall shrubs that can be grown, either in raised beds at the base of the walls or in pots.

To create an element of surprise

and a feeling of extended space, a central feature divides the garden into smaller interlinked spaces. The pivot of the layout is an ornamental pool with a tall stone fountain. It is surrounded by multilevel planting beds. An elegant statue provides a second focal point.

The pool and adjacent flower beds are set at 45° angles to the garden boundary, and the surrounding paths are also on the diagonal. This makes them proportionally longer than if they ran parallel to the boundaries and gives a feeling of generous width. The diagonals are repeated in the raised beds on the upper level,

---

▼ **Focal points** A softly playing fountain and a neoclassical statue are the two features that unite the multilevel planting beds and the low-lying patio. They also convey a sense of intimacy and seclusion behind foliage-covered walls.

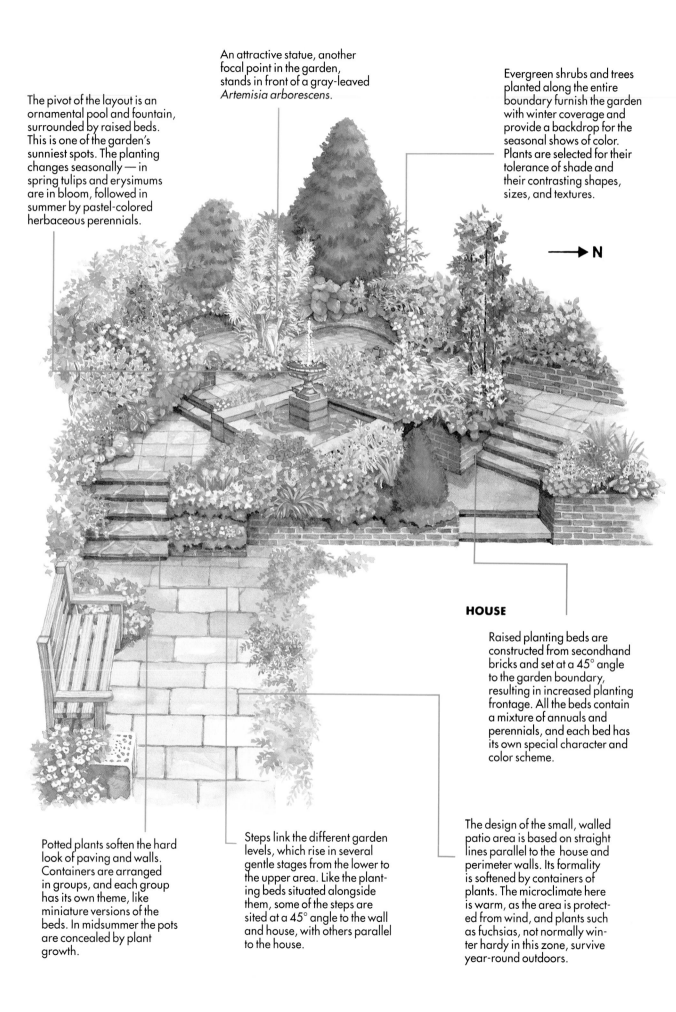

The pivot of the layout is an ornamental pool and fountain, surrounded by raised beds. This is one of the garden's sunniest spots. The planting changes seasonally — in spring tulips and erysimums are in bloom, followed in summer by pastel-colored herbaceous perennials.

An attractive statue, another focal point in the garden, stands in front of a gray-leaved *Artemisia arborescens*.

Evergreen shrubs and trees planted along the entire boundary furnish the garden with winter coverage and provide a backdrop for the seasonal shows of color. Plants are selected for their tolerance of shade and their contrasting shapes, sizes, and textures.

→ N

HOUSE

Raised planting beds are constructed from secondhand bricks and set at a 45° angle to the garden boundary, resulting in increased planting frontage. All the beds contain a mixture of annuals and perennials, and each bed has its own special character and color scheme.

Potted plants soften the hard look of paving and walls. Containers are arranged in groups, and each group has its own theme, like miniature versions of the beds. In midsummer the pots are concealed by plant growth.

Steps link the different garden levels, which rise in several gentle stages from the lower to the upper area. Like the planting beds situated alongside them, some of the steps are sited at a 45° angle to the wall and house, with others parallel to the house.

The design of the small, walled patio area is based on straight lines parallel to the house and perimeter walls. Its formality is softened by containers of plants. The microclimate here is warm, as the area is protected from wind, and plants such as fuchsias, not normally winter hardy in this zone, survive year-round outdoors.

▲ **Bird's-eye view** Seen from the balcony above, the garden becomes a feast of greenery and floral color, its geometric contours well concealed.

with increased frontage for planting as a result.

Walking through the garden, a visitor is presented with a series of changing vistas, as sharp corners are turned. The same small space is seen two or three times from slightly different viewpoints.

The garden is made more interesting by several levels that rise in gentle stages from the lower to the upper area. Short, shallow flights of steps connect the landings.

The paving of the lower area, which is a small patio, follows the straight lines of the house and boundary walls, offering a strong contrast to the plant forms. In the upper garden, the raised beds are laid out in two generous curves, springing from the diagonals, and these curves are reflected in the oval shape of the island bed. These curves separate the character of this area from that of the lower patio. They also help conceal the straight boundary walls and provide planting areas of varying depths.

Construction materials
Planning was key for this garden design. Locally obtained, second-hand bricks are used for the step risers and the retaining walls of the raised beds. The step treads and the pavement of the landings are cut from slabs of a grayish sandstone. The same stone is also used in the patio and upper area.

To raise the boundary walls, panels of wooden trellising have been installed. These furnish support for climbing plants — creating a vertical gardening space — and increase the privacy of the garden. The trellising is attached to steel rods, ½ in (1.2 cm) in diameter and 4½ ft (1.3 m) long. These rods were mounted by inserting them into 6 in (15 cm) holes drilled vertically along the top of the walls and at 4 ft (1.2 m) intervals. The trellising and the garden and house walls are painted white to reflect light, create an illusion of space, and provide a crisp, fresh backdrop for foliage and flowers.

Liberal amounts of bonemeal, dry cow manure, and peat moss were dug into the soil before any planting took place. Mulches and slow-acting fertilizers are applied as a topdressing each spring.

Planting
Bright floral displays are set against a soothing background of greenery, provided by permanent shrubs, conifers, and deciduous and evergreen climbers.

The beds are generally a mixture of permanent and temporary planting, but each bed has its own special character and a dominant color scheme, with minor cross-references to nearby beds. Because pale colors are more visible at night than deep ones, the main palette includes white, yellow, pink, and pale mauve. It is not inflexible, though, and a few red roses, for example, are grown for their sweet scent.

Evergreen shrubs and climbers furnish the garden, providing winter coverage and creating a setting for flowers. Various ivies, fatsia, and a hybrid between the two, × *Fatshedera lizei*, adorn the walls. There is a wide range of different leaf shapes, sizes, and textures, as well as a balance between variegated and plain leaves to add interest but not frenzy. Ever-gray shrubs include senecios, lavender, and the filigree-like *Artemisia arborescens*, planted around the base of the statue.

Plants are also selected for their tolerance of shade and less-than-perfect soil drainage. There are microclimatic variations within the garden, though, and the sunniest beds are given to roses, underplanted with tulips, primulas, and forget-me-nots in spring and with lime-green dwarf flowering

▲ **Microclimate** The small paved patio, enclosed by white walls and scented climbers, is sheltered at all times of year from the extremes of weather. Trailing fuchsias and impatiens add color to the greenery.

tobacco *(Nicotiana)* and green- and bronze-leaved wax begonias in summer.

The second sunniest bed, a 4 x 6 ft (1.2 x 1.8 m) rectangle by the pool, is a scaled-down herbaceous border. It contains phlox, campanula, and achillea, as well as an area for summer bedding. In spring the entire bed is filled with yellow erysimums and white lily-flowered tulips. In early summer there are pale blue petunias,

yellow and white snapdragons, and an edging of pink begonias.

In the shady, north-facing raised bed, in front of climbers and shrubs, erysimums thrive in spring. In summer this spot is filled with bedding plants such as tuberous-rooted begonias, tradescantias, and fancy-leaved begonias, which put on a magnificent display for several months. On the shady patio, pots of dwarf bamboo, daphne, evergreen euonymus, fatsia, and ivy thrive, along with cheerful white impatiens flowers.

Variation in plant height is also taken into consideration. In the flat beds a mounded effect is achieved by placing tall plants toward the middle of island beds or

at the back of borders along the walls. For high-level interest, in addition to the walls, there are two pergolas, one supporting wisteria and the other, ivy-leaved geranium *(Pelargonium peltatum)*. A balcony overlooking the patio is planted with hanging fuchsias, which trail gracefully and intermingle with branching ferns and climbing wall-trained roses.

There is also a balance between formality and informality: clipped boxwood hedging near the pool encloses a cheerful sprawl of hyacinths, tulips, and primroses in spring and impatiens in summer.

Philadelphus, lemon-scented verbena, and honeysuckle are grown for the strength of their scents. The heavily fragrant, pink-tinged *Jasminum polyanthum*, usually grown as a houseplant, thrives in the mild climate of this walled sunken garden. Similarly, hybrid fuchsias and ivy-leaved geraniums, usually too tender to overwinter outdoors in this zone, flourish here year-round and reach massive size.

There is no room in this garden for a lawn, but smooth mats of baby's tears *(Soleirolia soleirolii)* edge the small terraced beds rising immediately above the patio and transform them into tiers of green velvet. A variegated form of baby's tears neatly edges the island bed created at the base of the statue and serves as a soft foreground for the colorful spring and summer bedding plants that fill the bed.

Container planting
The patio relies on potted plants to soften the hard look of paving and walls. Containers of different sizes are grouped in tight clusters, and those at the back are raised on bricks to give some extra height. By midsummer the pots are concealed by the plant growth.

Some containers are double planted — for example, with early-flowering regal lilies and late-flowering speciosum lilies, to give a display that lasts from midsummer to early fall.

Plant care
For such plants to grow luxuriantly and beautifully in succession in the crowded, unnatural environment of an urban garden, they must be given large amounts of food and water. The plants receive an annual feeding of bonemeal,

▲ **Shade lovers** Each planting bed uses permanent and temporary plants to articulate a separate theme, emphasizing foliage color, form, and texture. Shade-loving plants include caladiums, with their marbled white-and-green leaves, and an edging of dark green hostas. Wax begonias and impatiens also thrive in shade, their pastel colors becoming luminous at night.

◄ **Formal pool** The small garden pool has a classic shape and is in perfect proportion with the rest of the garden. Sited in a sunny part, it is the pivot of the whole design and, together with the fountain, introduces an air of tranquillity. The adjacent bed is brightened by pale-colored tulips and scented erysimums in spring and perennials and bedding plants in summer.

and a slow-release organic fertilizer is applied in early summer and midsummer. The roses are also fertilized twice a year with a specially formulated rose food. Container plants are fed regularly with a soluble houseplant fertilizer.

Regular and generous watering is necessary, both because raised beds and containers dry out quickly and because the house and garden walls create a rain shadow.

There is a great deal of repetitive seasonal gardening. Spring-flowering bulbs and biennials are planted in fall, then removed and replaced with annuals in late spring. These are in turn dug up and discarded in fall, except for tuberous-rooted begonias, which are lifted, dried off, and stored over winter.

▶ **Summer highlights** The green-clad high walls by the patio are studded in summer with splashes of color from hanging baskets of trailing fuchsias. They do well in shade, and in a sheltered environment survive most winters in the open.

▼ **Spring color** The diagonal layout and multilevel design make the garden look larger than it is, particularly in spring, when growth is in the early stages.

SMALL PAVED GARDENS

**A garden floor made from paving may be
the only practical solution in a heavily used confined
garden — and it is virtually maintenance free.**

In small gardens where foot traffic is heavy, grass may not survive. Paving is more practical and offers an ideal means of visually linking different features. It can also distract the eye from the confinement of the site. The small garden described here manages to convey a sense of intimacy and privacy yet does not feel enclosed. This is partly due to its strong architectural framework, partly to its clever design, and partly to the horticultural skill of its owner, who has brought the whole composition to vibrant life.

The framework
The owner started with very little apart from a basic rectangular framework of walls and buildings, enclosing an area of about 200 sq yd/m. The main house sits squarely at one end of the plot; opposite this, no more than 33 ft (10 m) away and on a slightly lower level, lies an old carriage house that has been sensitively converted into a guest house. Stone walls define the remaining boundaries of the garden.

The ground drops a little to one side of the guest house to form a small, secluded area.

Paving and steps
Paved surfaces, such as paths and patios, are the "bones" of any garden design. In a small garden, simplicity is all-important — many a garden has been ruined by using too many conflicting patterns and surfaces. The temptation to clutter a design is great, as paving comes in many colors, textures, and sizes of stone, tile, and cast blocks. But if there is too much variation, the floor of the "outside room" can quickly become a visual jumble.

Paving material should be chosen to harmonize with the surrounding buildings. With a brick house, for example, a brick paved patio connects the garden to the house. Similarly, the courtyard of an old farmhouse might appropriately be paved with stone flags or cobblestone.

With modern houses the choice

▼ **Miniature lawn** Baby's tears *(Soleirolia soleirolii)* makes an unusual substitute for grass in a shady and damp area. However, it is invasive and needs frequent trimming.

A small secret garden fits neatly into the slight change of level at the side of the guest rooms. This small space is itself divided in two. Next to the building lies a tiny sunken courtyard, paved with stone block and furnished with pots and ornaments. Beyond the sunken courtyard is a delightful little water feature set in a niche in the stone wall.

Curving, gently meandering paths encourage dawdling and close scrutiny of the surrounding plants. The plants are allowed to encroach on the paths, with hardly any hindrance, heightening the general feeling of informality and subtly blending the hard and soft landscaping elements.

A secluded paved sitting area in the center of the garden is wrapped around with a soft, open circle of foliage planting, which provides both shelter and privacy. The entrance to the central sitting area is like a doorway leading the eye forward. From the opposite side, it directs attention back to the main house.

An old carriage house has been converted into a separate guest cottage. The main house sits squarely at the other end of the lot, not more than 33 ft (10 m) away. Stone walls form the garden's remaining boundaries.

▲ **Granite floor** Blocks laid in regular courses follow gentle curves. They are time-consuming to lay, but once in place, they are maintenance free and virtually indestructible.

Granite blocks laid in distinct courses, like brickwork, create strong parallel lines that lead the eye from side to side, making the garden appear larger than it really is. The symmetrically laid granite blocks seem to drift into the plantings on either side.

may not be quite this obvious. Materials (ideally no more than two in any composition) should be chosen that complement the house.

This garden relies on granite blocks to echo an element of stonework in the house, as well as provide a mellow and uniform background.

The way in which paving, of whatever kind, is laid can make a considerable difference to the look of a garden. Here the granite blocks have been laid in distinct courses, like brickwork. This design produces strong parallel lines that lead the eye from side to side, opening the garden up and helping to increase the feeling of space.

This effect is reinforced by steps running the full width of the garden and fronting the patio by the house. If these had been positioned differently, the overall sense of unity and spaciousness would have been considerably weakened.

In a walled garden, it is very important to create a feeling of

spaciousness. Although walls provide privacy and a useful support for climbing plants, they can also tend to have an unwanted claustrophobic effect. As a rule, paths usually improve matters, giving a sense of movement and of going places.

A straight path encourages brisk walking, which is undesirable in a small lot. In this garden the paths curve and meander gently, encouraging the visitor to linger and observe the surrounding plants. Curves help to release a garden from its linear contours.

Two paths run along either side of the garden, linking the buildings and giving a good view of the borders at the boundary walls. Cleverly laid, the granite blocks seem to drift into the plantings on either side, while the plants are allowed to spill naturally onto the paths, unrestrained by staking. This increases the feeling of informality and

subtly blends the masonry with soft plantings.

Planning for privacy

An open, paved sitting area in the center of the garden is softly encircled by foliage planting, creating a feeling of seclusion.

While the central sitting area is the pivot of the garden, there is also room for a secondary focal point, a small "secret garden," which fits neatly into the slight change of level at the side of the guest rooms.

This small space, bounded by a stone wall on one side, has its own courtyard lined with granite blocks and furnished with stone ornaments and plant pots.

Bright green baby's tears (*Soleirolia soleirolii*) occupies the center of the tiny courtyard and creeps along the drystone wall. Like the accompanying ferns and trailing ivy, baby's tears thrives in shade but can grow out of

▲ **Stone baskets** Classic stone ornaments, lavishly embellished with fruits and flowers, define the perimeters of the central sitting area. They are backed by clumps of feathery, bright pink cosmos.

control unless regularly trimmed.

Beyond the sunken courtyard and hidden from the path by planting, a delightful little water feature is set in a niche in the old stone wall. Although this makes use of a natural spring, a similar feature could be built into any garden, fed by a submersible pump in a pool.

This pretty feature is screened by foliage, so it remains hidden until the last moment — it is a surprise at the end of the path.

Both these enclosed spaces, or "gardens within gardens" — the large central area and the small sunken courtyard — distract the eye from the strict rectangular boundaries and help to create a sense of spaciousness.

Planting plans

While a strong basic structure and a well-integrated layout are both essential to good garden design, it is the planting that brings the whole composition to life.

The choice of plants is a question of personal taste, but success is more likely with planning and restraint than with random decisions. Most gardeners want some background color and year-round interest; they also aim to keep maintenance costs and effort down to reasonable levels. Shrubs and hardy perennials are less labor-intensive than beds of annual flowers.

Many people assume, quite wrongly, that the more plants you have, the harder it is to keep order in a garden. In fact, the opposite is true — a well-stocked garden and good ground cover allow weeds little room to develop.

In this garden the planting has been skillfully planned to provide interest across the seasons. The species have been carefully chosen, as much for foliage texture, color, and size as for flowers.

In late summer the invaluable flowers of Japanese anemones (*Anemone japonica*), phlox, mallows, and hydrangeas blend into a background of grasses, bamboos, hostas, and *Fatsia japonica*.

Heights and shapes are cleverly juxtaposed — a clump-forming dwarf hebe, with its narrow glossy green leaves and racemes of white summer flowers, contrasts with feathery silver artemisia and the quill-like leaves of fescues (*Festuca*), ornamental perennial grasses. The bold, sculptural leaves of *Hosta sieboldiana* or *Hosta* 'Albomarginata' make a perfect foil for ferns and the evergreen arrow bamboo (*Pseudosasa japonica*).

Ideally, flower colors should harmonize with each other. Hot, strong colors — red, orange, and mauve — demand instant attention and can overpower softer shades, but they are useful in small groups to provide emphasis and contrast amid foliage plants. The flowers in this garden are mainly in pastel shades, with pink, soft purple, and white playing predominant roles.

Annuals — raised at home from seed or purchased at the

▲ **Planting themes** The sitting area is enclosed by repeat planting on either side. Shrubs include mounds of hebe, blue-flowered *Ceanothus thyrsiflorus*, white *Hydrangea paniculata*, and pink *Abelia* x *grandiflora*.

▼ **Shades of pink** Late summer brings a froth of pink from shrubby *Lavatera olbia* 'Rosea' and the tall spikes of *Lythrum salicaria* 'Firecandle.' Later still, the pale green heads of *Sedum* 'Autumn Joy' turn russet-red.

garden center — are useful for quick color, filling odd soil pockets, and providing cut flowers. They are indispensable as a garden takes shape and before the more permanent plants fill out their allotted space.

Maintenance is always necessary, if only to prevent shrubs, hardy perennials, and annuals from overrunning each other. The temptation may be to let things grow as they will, without too much pruning, but a more ruthless approach must be adopted if you want to retain an attractive balance of flowers and foliage.

Many of the species planted here — including cotinus, viburnum, hydrangea, and bamboo — would soon outgrow their allotted positions if not kept in check.

If a plant dislikes persistent cutting back or fails to thrive, dig it out and replace it with another species or temporarily fill the gap with annuals.

Ornaments and furniture
Choose garden furniture and ornaments to harmonize with surrounding plants and hardscape. A lightweight table and chairs are just right in this particular garden. Ornamental stone baskets, filled with stone fruit and flowers, echo stonework elsewhere in the garden.

Solid granite spheres are good for visual impact. Historically, such ornaments were placed on top of gateposts, supposedly to ward off bad luck.

In the final analysis, it is the sense of discipline and careful choice that make even the tiniest garden work well. Everything should look right for its place and be perfectly in proportion to the allotted space, as is true here.

Granite blocks
Often (though incorrectly) referred to as cobblestones, these roughly shaped chunks of granite were once used for street paving. They are difficult to obtain now, but you may be able to buy them from a local stoneyard, especially if you live near an older city. Because of their small size, such blocks are ideal for use in a free-form design — they can easily be laid to follow a curve.

This type of paving, however, is costly, and meticulous workmanship is necessary if the resulting surface is to be flat and even.

▲ **Granite spheres** Perfect globes punctuate the lush planting of purple and variegated shrubs.

▼ **Cool retreat** Foliage plants of contrasting shapes, textures, and colors furnish a quiet corner of the garden.

Designs for large gardens

Large gardens — in the city, suburbs, or country — present a special challenge as well as endless possibilities. Without a carefully designed plan, they can become a series of separate activity centers that bear little or no relation to each other. The topography and exposure strongly influence the potential layout. In hilly, windswept situations, the necessary shelterbelts force the design to look inward, while a garden with views over the sea, rolling countryside, or a distant mountain range can visually extend outward beyond its actual boundaries.

The most successful designs for large gardens are simple and uncomplicated, with shapes relating to the geometry of the house and its surroundings. Views from the house — from the front or back door and from principal windows — should dictate the main axis of the landscape plan. Your convenience and the realities of the natural landform should dictate the placement of features such as changes in level and raised beds, and structures such as a pergola or an ornamental pool.

Maintaining a large garden can be a challenge, but thoughtful planning and planting can cut the workload by confining labor-intensive planting to the area right around the house. Plant the outer areas with low-maintenance turf and groupings of trees and shrubs.

Rural view Leaf-shrouded walls and mounds of foliage plants blend easily with the rural landscape.

FORMAL COUNTRY GARDENS

**Generally, gardens in the country are larger
and more labor-intensive than those in cities and suburbs.
A bold design can cut maintenance to a minimum.**

Next to this L-shaped house with brightly painted trim is a dazzling courtyard area, ablaze with color during the summer. It forms a wide stage, from which uninterrupted views lead to large and tranquil lawns with island beds of sculpted conifers.

In a deliberate effort to invigorate an already-established garden, the immediate area around the house was redesigned as a large courtyard with many planting beds. The result is a separate flower garden enclosed by low brick walls. Strong demarcation lines work well only in large gardens. Because of the large expanse of lawns and established island beds, the transition from colorful intimacy to a more formal layout appears natural.

The courtyard area has been given a patchwork effect, with flagstone paths running at right angles to the house, interspersed with gravel-mulched beds and more flagstone paving. When broken up by bright flower color, the various stone surfaces offer a good contrast to the soft and tranquil green background provided by the garden's lawns, trees, and shrubs. A low wall, built in brick to match the house, partly encloses the courtyard and marks the boundary between the outdoor living room and the garden proper.

Climbers and wall shrubs

The picturesque cottage-style house is enhanced by shrubs and creepers that partly cover the house and merge with the triangular gravel bed. Over the porch is a flowering honeysuckle (*Lonicera periclymenum*), and along the east-facing wall is an ornamental quince (*Chaenomeles speciosa*), its bright spring blossoms followed by small, edible golden yellow fruits.

Persian ivy (*Hedera colchica*) covers part of the south-facing wall of the house and trails down, skirting the mound of *Cotoneaster horizontalis* and rooting where it touches the ground between the rounded shapes of large lavender bushes.

The lavender flourishes in this sunny corner; a few plants have even seeded themselves between gaps in the paving stones and farther away in the graveled beds. Another self-seeder is valerian (*Centranthus ruber*), in both the red and white forms. It is a prolific plant for open, sunny sites and thrives in the poorest of soils.

Purple campanulas and pale-colored sun roses (*Helianthemum*)

▼ **Planting beds** A patchwork of low-growing shrubs and perennials is crisscrossed by flagstone paths and pockets of gravel. Hanging baskets and wall climbers provide a measure of vertical color and interest.

spill onto the paths and break up the graveled areas. The pink flowers of thyme and the brilliant blue of speedwell *(Veronica austriaca teucrium)* provide lively splashes of color. The blues have the added attraction of echoing and enhancing the deep blue of the house doors and window frames.

Color is also provided by numerous pastel-shaded geraniums, some with variegated leaves, growing in square, round, and columnar terra-cotta pots and hanging baskets.

Garden ornaments — a large stone mushroom by the house and a sundial by the far end of the path — give more structure to the slightly raised paved area. A hollow tree stump houses pots of ivy-leaved and fancy-leaved zonal geraniums and impatiens. It effortlessly guides the view from

▶ **Change of pace** Shallow brick steps mark the level changes and the transition between paving and gravel surfaces. They echo the color of the house and the low walls that enclose the courtyard area.

▼ **Color harmony** Pinks and blues, blending in with the mellow red-brick of the house walls and the blue-painted trim, are the predominant colors in the summer season.

Flagstones, graveled beds, and low brick walls divide a brilliantly colorful display of small flowering shrubs, perennials, and potted plants from the mature garden beyond. Decorative pots, a sundial, and a planted tree stump provide additional interest. The house walls are clothed with ivies and honeysuckle, and hanging baskets overflow with summer color.

A golden yew — clipped square — forms the focal point in a large bed of mixed conifers and shrubs. The conifers, which display great variety of texture, form, and color, are set off by a narrow edging of red begonias. The strong contrast between this bed and the flowers near the house is particularly dramatic.

A rustic pergola arches over a path of flagstones and leads the eye away from the intimate planting near the house and out into other parts of the garden. The brick supports for the pergola echo both the brick of the house and the low brick walls surrounding the courtyard.

An oblong bed contains mixed shrubs and perennials. It carries the color theme from the main flower planting out into the green expanse of lawn.

A second conifer and a bed of mixed shrubs complement the adjacent island bed. Both beds are easily maintained and provide a restful contrast to the vivid colors of the courtyard and the house.

▲ **Island beds** A golden yew, clipped square at the top, offers a startling contrast to the dark green conifers, becoming an arresting focal point away from the courtyard's kaleidoscope of colors.

▼ **Welcome gestures** Hanging baskets, sweetly scented honeysuckle, twining clematis, and clumps of lavender adorn the entrance and soften the hard surfaces of flagstone and brick.

ground level to the vertical expanse of climbers.

The triangular brick insets in the paved area, together with the bricks confining the flower beds, subtly link this whole area with the brick of the house. Such small features are worth the investment of time and thought because they unify this garden area, making it a coherent whole.

The entire paved area is demarcated from the rest of the garden by low brick walls. Despite the lack of height — there are no raised beds or significant changes of level in this area — there is a feeling of intimacy closely associated with the house. The south-facing brick wall shelters a narrow border planted with thrift (*Armeria maritima*), aubrieta, and hollyhocks, giving a distinctly cottage garden atmosphere to this sunny corner.

The courtyard area curves out in the center, between the low brick walls, to a border of rounded shrubs that form an edging to the lawn. Among them are two excellent robust ground-cover shrubs — the vigorous, low-growing, scarlet-berried *Cotoneaster dammeri* and the more rounded evergreen *Viburnum tinus*, with pink-budded white flowers in late winter and early spring, followed

by clusters of blue to black berries in the fall.

Conifer islands
A spectacular effect has been created in this garden by two large
conifer beds and by individual
specimen plants set into the lawn.
One bed has a sculptural effect,
with a 10 ft (3 m) high, square-
clipped golden English yew (*Taxus baccata* 'Aurea') in striking
contrast with the dark green yel-
low-tipped foliage of a western
red cedar *(Thuja plicata)* and a
yellow-flowered potentilla. The
whole bed — brilliant in its contrasting foliage colors, shapes,
and leaf textures — is set off by
an edging of bright red bedding
begonias.

There is an especially good
view of this bed from the east side
of the house. With lupines and
poppies in the foreground, the
vista reaches beyond the sundial
to the large conifer bed on one
side and to another conifer bed
and a well-clipped mature beech
hedge on the other side. Other at-
tractions in the lawn include a
Norway spruce *(Picea abies)* and
a triangular framework of stout
rustic poles set into a small circular bed. A yellow rose ('Climbing
Allgold') clambers up this framework, partnered by the large-
flowered *Clematis* 'Dr. Ruppel'
(deep pink with carmine stripes
and golden stamens).

The island beds of conifers and
shrubs are a permanent framework that stays much the same

▲ **Pillar rose** A rustic
framework supports an
attractive combination of
climbers — the yellow *Rosa*
'Climbing Allgold' and the
large-flowered, pink-red
Clematis 'Dr. Ruppel.'
Both respond well to hard
pruning in late winter.

◄ **Color contrast** The large
island bed of golden and dark
green conifers appears all
the more impressive as it rises
from a footing of bright red
wax begonias.

all year. These green islands of
rest and tranquillity offset the
busy, changing colors of the courtyard flower beds. The bold, formal shape of the square-clipped
yew, immediately catching the
eye, gives some zest to the foliage
planting. Yew is ideal for molding
into large architectural shapes
but grows very slowly, so it takes
time to become bulky enough to
cut to the desired outline.

The evergreens are fairly easy
to maintain — just an occasional
trimming for shape and size —
and the lawn, with its broad,
sweeping curves, is easy to mow.
The beech hedge needs one annual trim, in mid- to late summer. It
retains attractive brown leaves
through winter. By design, all the
labor-intensive gardening is concentrated in the flower beds and
borders near the house.

▶ **Unusual container** A hollowed-out tree
stump, replete with moss-covered edges,
holds pot-grown zonal and ivy-leaved
geraniums. It brings welcome height to
an otherwise low planting plan.

▼**Evergreen cover** Persian ivy *(Hedera
colchica)* clothes a house wall in green
and gold; it trails around window frames
and among *Cotoneaster horizontalis*
before reaching the ground.

COUNTRY CONTEMPORARY

**House style will always influence garden
design, and the surrounding landscape can offer
challenges as well as opportunities.**

For many gardeners the challenge of creating privacy in a suburban or urban environment is of overriding importance. In open countryside, however, the problem is reversed, and gardeners seek to open up views to the rural landscape. The garden described here achieves a balance between the stark geometry of a modern A-frame house and its surrounding hilly landscape. The site is near the sea, so barriers against the prevailing winds are needed to protect plantings from salt-laden sprays.

The site
In this windswept, hilly, and open landscape, the house and new garden lie in an isolated spot, amid fields. The garden is nearly level and covers approximately 27,000 sq ft (2,500 sq m).

Mature trees nearby form a leafy backdrop, providing vertical interest on a grand scale. The soil is well drained.

The layout
The owners wanted an attractive, well-designed landscape, with a wide range of plants, and were prepared to maintain it properly. The garden had to be tough as well as attractive so that young children could enjoy it too.

The layout is simple — an expanse of lawn with ornamental beds and borders surrounding the house and hugging the garden boundaries. The beds and borders close to the house are rigidly geometric, reflecting the stark lines of the house itself; those farther away are more sweeping and informal in plan, offering a transition from cultivated garden to farm fields and a wild landscape.

Next to the house is a sheltered south-facing patio that offers extensive views of the garden as well as the surrounding countryside. Flagstone paving connects the patio and various entrances to the house. It is laid in straight but staggered lines to reflect the style of the house and to create planting beds. At the edge the

---

▼ **Rural prospects** On the sheltered side, the low informal planting backed by a rustic fence allows uninterrupted views from the house and the patio across rolling fields and woodland.

▲ **Ground cover** A large planting bed on the patio is filled with foliage plants, including such ornamental grasses as white-striped gardener's garters (*Phalaris arundinacea* 'Picta') and low clumps of blue fescue (*Festuca glauca*). Thyme creeps among cracks in the paving, and above it all stands a luxuriant tree of heaven.

On the sheltered southern side, the boundary is marked only by post-and-rail fencing and low-growing perennials so as not to impede the wide views over rolling fields and woodland.

Tough, wind-resistant cluster pines (*Pinus pinaster*) are planted as specimen trees in the lawn to filter the wind and provide year-round interest. These pines thrive in sandy soil.

The neatly mowed lawn spreads a green carpet around the house and the borders. It sets off the flower colors and leaf forms and contrasts with the fields beyond.

Shelterbelts of cotoneaster, elaeagnus, and olearia protect the northern, eastern, and western boundaries from salt-laden sea spray. They are themselves shielded by a wind barrier of mature trees outside the garden.

Flagstone paving, laid in a geometric pattern that complements the architecture of the house, surrounds the house. The large surface is broken up by several planting beds and softened with creeping plants and sprawling foliage.

The patio faces due south and is sheltered by the house. It is ideal as an outdoor living room in summer and enjoys extensive views across the garden to the rural surroundings.

paving is flush with the lawn to facilitate mowing.

Salt-laden winds are a potential threat to the plantings, so the northern, eastern, and western garden boundaries are planted with tough screening plants. The southern boundary, which is naturally sheltered and overlooks grainfields and an apple orchard, is demarcated with low post-and-rail fencing in keeping with the agricultural landscape. Clumps of perennials — achilleas, oxeye daisies, and campanulas — frame the view.

Planting design

Plants are the major feature, and a wide range of planting enlivens the simple layout. Most of the plants are popular, ordinary ones that are widely available.

The selection is pleasingly varied, with trees, shrubs, and perennials. Old-fashioned cottage garden plants include pinks *(Dianthus),* Jacob's ladder *(Polemonium),* and yellow loosestrife *(Lysimachia).* Such brilliantly colored blossoms show up well in the bright seaside sun. The main criteria for choosing these plants are

▲ **Architectural flair** Plant silhouettes break the rigid angles of the house. A white birch rustles above green laurel bushes and yellow-flowered St.-John's-wort *(Hypericum calycinum).*

toughness, a strong visual character, and a contribution to the overall texture of the garden.

In successful garden designs, all the plants are positioned so as to furnish the maximum contrast of form, foliage, and color. Foliage is as important as flowers, and this garden contains a wonderful

88

mixture of foliage: spiky, lacy, rounded, glossy, furry, variegated, and many shades of green.

Ornamental grasses, such as miscanthus, blue fescue, and green- and white-striped gardener's-garters, are a feature, along with variegated ground elder, a sophisticated cultivar of the dreaded and invasive weed. In late winter and spring naturalized bulbs sprout color; in summer and fall, roses, daylilies, poppies, alstroemerias, and New England asters flower.

Near the patio and paving, low-growing plants are grouped in dense clumps, mounds, and carpets of ground cover. Here and there they are encouraged to spill onto the paving, softening the right-angled geometry of the design. Tiny creepers make their way along cracks between paving stones, which are laid without grouting.

There is a rough gradation in

▲ **Cluster pines** Thriving in mild coastal areas, these mature trees bear brown cones that remain on the trees for years.

▼ **Fields in summer** Spikes of yellow loosestrife and New England asters merge into the fields of ripening grain.

heights, from low at the edge of the planting to high by the house. Trees provide most of the high-level interest.

A young ailanthus rises out of a large planting bed on the patio. *Ailanthus altissima*, or tree of heaven, is commonly considered an urban weed; in a rural setting as here, however, it is less invasive and makes a very fast-growing, hardy deciduous tree. If cut back, as here, it forms a graceful multistemmed tree with ashlike leaves as much as 3½ ft (1.1 m) long. Female trees bear long bunches of yellow-red keylike fruits in summer.

When mature, the ailanthus will become the pivotal point of the whole garden; the house may even seem to have been planned around it. A multistemmed cut-leaved sumac makes another strong focal point in an island bed on the north side of the house.

The lawn is neatly mowed. It has been left uncluttered in the center to increase the sense of space, with specimen conifers sited near the flower borders that line the garden's perimeter.

The color scheme

Green is the predominant color and provides a cool framework for vivid splashes of bright yellow, purple, red, and blue. Even slightly garish colors — such as that of the floribunda rose 'Orange Sensation' — fit in well.

Color is used in bold groups and drifts among the background

green rather than being splashed around randomly. By the patio, pastel shades predominate, while the stronger colors are reserved for the outer borders.

Coastal climate

Because the winter climate is comparatively warm in this area, frost-sensitive plants — such as eucalyptus, olearia (the white-flowered daisybush that revels in coastal climates), New Zealand flax *(Phormium tenax)*, and the yellow-flowered *Pittosporum tobira*, with its heavy orange scent — are planted as permanent features outdoors. (In cooler regions, these can be grown in large containers and moved to shelter for the winter.)

Even the spike dracaena *(Cordyline australis)*, planted as a lawn specimen near the patio, will survive most winters here.

▲ **Windbreaks** Tough evergreen shrubs of cotoneaster, elaeagnus, and olearia create a dense barrier to block salt-laden winds from the sea. As shelterbelts, evergreen plants are more effective than walls or fences.

◄ **Color points** The bright blooms of *Rosa* 'Orange Sensation' are subtly toned down by the dark green leaf fans of New Zealand flax *(Phormium tenax)*.

Cluster pines and junipers are part of the natural vegetation of the area; both the species and their more sophisticated cultivars are used in the planting. Pines are set out as small specimen trees on the lawn, singly and in groups; they will fill out with time.

Dwarf pines in the flower beds and borders provide year-round color, especially important when the herbaceous plants are dormant. Junipers, both upright and horizontal, contribute further evergreen interest to the borders.

What is omitted from this modern garden is as important as what is included. There are no patterns of bedding plants or other short-lived plants that require frequent replacement. There are no statues, pools, fountains, flower pots, or urns. The house and the garden plants are allowed to speak for themselves.

SUBURBAN GARDENS

**On a suburban lot, a garden design
based on plants with strong visual impact
throughout the year is all-important.**

A well-designed suburban garden can be as beautiful in its own way as that of a country estate. This garden transforms a rectangular front yard that ends at the street and has a driveway on the side. It contains the usual components of a suburban garden: hedges at the property lines, a lawn, and beds with evergreen and deciduous shrubs, bulbs, and perennials.

What sets this garden apart from the ordinary is the rich variety of plants. The owners are avid plant collectors who offer surprises in the plantings, giving the garden a memorable character. Another special quality is the use of space: not a single inch is wasted, yet no plant is crowded.

The layout
The garden, which is 70 x 35 ft (21 x 10.5 m), faces north but is fortunately still sunny. It has an open, airy feeling, with only the area immediately outside the house in shade. The site slopes gently away from the house and is sheltered by the hedges and a neighboring house. The soil is well drained, acid, and sandy. The mature hedges of mixed conifers, weigela, laurel, and privet are kept pruned well back to give the most space.

The owners, who enjoy growing plants from seeds and cuttings, wanted to display their vast collection without creating a museumlike landscape. This design, with its S-shaped lawn, sets off the plants nicely.

Between the lawn and the driveway a narrow island bed has been created for conifers. A path leading from the driveway to the front door divides the peat bog garden in front of the house from the mixed flower border opposite. A semiwild mixed border is set along the yard's front edge.

The peat bog garden
The owners like ericaceous plants (members of the rhododendron family) and have turned a shady corner by the house into a haven for them. The soil was first excavated to a depth of 1 ft (30 cm) and mixed with sphagnum peat and composted leaves to help keep the soil moist. The excavation was then lined with perforated black

---

▼ **Suburban garden** A traditional layout includes lawn, paths, beds, mixed borders, and specimen trees. However, the choice of plants can lift a garden from the average to the unique throughout the changing seasons.

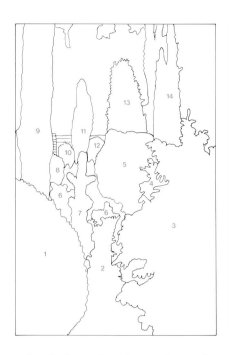

CONIFER BED

A wide variety of conifers, from pencil-slim to mound-shaped and from soft gold to blue-gray, bring visual interest throughout all seasons of the year as well as extending a degree of privacy to the garden. The plan identifies some of the main conifers in the collection.

1 Golden dwarf arborvitae (*Thuja occidentalis* 'Rheingold')
2 Columbine (*Aquilegia vulgaris*)
3 Norway spruce (*Picea abies* 'Acrocona')
4 Lawson cypress (*Chamaecyparis lawsoniana* 'Lane')
5 Dwarf Sawara cypress (*Chamaecyparis pisifera*)

6 Prostrate noble fir (*Abies procera* 'Glauca Prostrata')
7 Bristle-cone pine (*Pinus aristata*)
8 Japanese cedar (*Cryptomeria japonica* 'Spiralis')
9 Irish juniper (*Juniperus communis* 'Hibernica')
10 Lawson cypress (*Chamaecyparis lawsoniana* 'Ellwood's Gold')
11 Golden Irish yew (*Taxus baccata* 'Fastigiata Aureomarginata')
12 Dwarf Sawara cypress (*Chamaecyparis pisifera* 'Squarrosa Sulphurea')
13 Golden arborvitae (*Thuja occidentalis* 'Lutea')
14 Rocky Mountain juniper (*Juniperus scopulorum* 'Skyrocket')

polyethylene sheeting and gravel. A 1 ft (30 cm) high wall was erected around the bed and the soil mixture returned to the excavation to form a raised peat bog garden.

Acid-loving species from North America, Asia, and Europe are grown here. The main season of display is spring, but some color brightens up other seasons as well, such as snowdrops in winter and brilliant blue gentians in fall.

Masses of dwarf rhododendrons fill the peat garden with color from midspring to early summer, with pieris and dwarf shrubs, such as cranberries, and the slender-stemmed bog rosemary (*Andromeda polifolia*).

There are no true heathers, but in this garden the related mountain heathers (*Phyllodoce*) carpet the soil with their narrow, dark green leaves and bell-like flowers.

The moist, cool, acid soil and shade are ideal for herbaceous and bulbous woodland plants, such as dog-tooth violets (*Erythronium*) and trilliums. Wood anemones, purple-leaved violets, and hardy cyclamens enjoy the same conditions. There are also several terrestrial orchids, including yellow lady's slipper, and clumps of deciduous ferns.

Single- and double-flowered *Sanguinaria* plants are grown for their ruffled leaves and waxy white spring flowers. Their common name, "bloodroot," comes from the distinctive red sap the plants exude when cut. Pale blue hepaticas, resembling the anemones to which they are related, provide spring color at the same time as snowdrops.

Here, too, thrives the jack-in-the-pulpit (*Arisaema triphyllum*),

a woodland plant, whose early-summer flowers are borne on a spike inside a white-veined, purple-brown hood.

The conifer bed

The owners wanted a range of conifers. Because of limited space, they chose examples of each type: pencil- or mound-shaped, horizontal or dwarf, in a range of contrasting colors.

Many were grown from cuttings or transplanted from the gardens of friends; others were bought or traded through plant societies such as the American Rock Garden Society (check your public library for a directory listing local chapters).

Spacing trees and shrubs at a distance suitable to their ultimate spread can leave a garden looking bare for years. Here, the owners decided to space the conifers according to medium-term rather than long-term growth. A few conifers, potentially too big for the garden, were included for their unique appeal.

After a couple of decades, the conifer bed is pleasantly full, but a lot of discreet pruning is needed during the growing season. When pruning cannot contain a plant without disfiguring it, the plant is carefully dug up (in fall), its roots

◀ **Raised peat garden** Cool, moist, acid soil is essential for the rhododendrons that burst into glorious bloom in late spring. It also suits heaths and heathers, dog-tooth violets, and woodland plants like trilliums and wood anemones.

▲ **Slim conifers** Slender junipers
and Irish yews retain their narrowly
columnar shapes well into maturity,
with a minimum of pruning. They add
vertical interest to small beds, and the
golden forms create focal points.

◄ **Leaf contrasts** The spear-shaped
leaves of *Arum italicum italicum*,
marbled gray and green, are in stark
contrast to the near-yellow foliage of
Hosta fortunei 'Albo-picta.' In the background the feathery-leaved peonies
are a modest presence.

▶ **Open-plan garden** In spite of dense
planting, the garden feels open and airy,
as there are no obvious boundaries. An
annual mulch of shredded bark keeps
the soil cool and weed free.

balled and burlapped, then given
to friends. This allows time for
the roots to become established
before the cold weather.

Shearing back fast-growing
conifers, such as columnar *Cupressus macrocarpa* 'Gold-crest,'
keeps them compact and dense;
in the case of this conifer it also
encourages production of the rich
golden, feathery juvenile foliage.

It is also a good idea to pinch
back the growing tips of slow-
growing conifers all through the

growing season. Though time-consuming, this bonsailike practice results in dense branching and a compact but exaggerated form.

Slender, pencil-shaped conifers are a special feature of the garden. *Juniperus communis* 'Hibernica' and *J. scopulorum* 'Skyrocket' are particularly valuable since they retain their slim shapes naturally.

Border plants

The mixed border is dominated by a golden honey locust (*Gleditsia triacanthos inermis* 'Sunburst'), which starts the season with a bright golden glow. The border also contains a yellow-flowered tree peony, *Elaeagnus × ebbingei,* and variegated pittosporum. The shrubs are underplanted with clumps of hostas, poppies, and daylilies.

In calling the unirrigated bed near the road the "semiwild garden," the owners are referring not so much to the type of plants but to their style of maintenance. Here, such bulbs as crocuses (especially *Crocus tomasinianus*), alliums, colchicums, daffodils, and tulips multiply undisturbed. Mat-forming silver artemisias and the golden form of creeping Jenny (*Lysimachia nummularia* 'Aurea') provide later cover.

There are masses of rudbeckias and New England asters for late-summer color. Shrubs include the smoke tree *(Cotinus coggygria)* and yellow-leaved *Berberis thunbergii* 'Aurea.'

▲ **Ordered wilderness** Bulbs in the border are left to multiply and come up year after year. Pink and white tulips and clumps of white-flowered ornamental onions (*Allium*) poke through a golden ground cover of creeping Jenny (*Lysimachia nummularia* 'Aurea').

◄ **Good companions** Thoughtful planning results in fine combinations of complementary forms and colors. Central to this group is a clump of spiky blue oat grass (*Helictotrichon sempervirens*) partnered by a creamy yellow peony and, on the right, the bright foliage of *Spiraea japonica* 'Goldflame.' On the left is a golden dwarf conifer (*Chamaecyparis pisifera* 'Filifera Aurea').

AWKWARD SITES

Intrusive structures can be difficult to disguise, but with imaginative design and careful planting they can become attractive features.

All too often people treat their gardens simply as single-level enclosures of unrelated features, but a unified three-dimensional approach is often much more rewarding. This is especially true when dealing with a difficult, angular-shaped garden with unappealing architectural elements. By using a range of design techniques and well-chosen plants, hard, obtrusive vertical lines can be altered and intrusive structures disguised or incorporated into the overall layout.

The garden shown here is designed to improve an awkward, irregularly shaped space that has a garage in one corner and a conservatory in another.

Creating unity

The problem of large, dominant shapes within a flat, rectangular lot has been overcome by designing the garden on three distinct but linked levels and by turning an intrusive garage into an attractive feature.

The garden's large central area is emphasized by the sweeping curves of a lawn that begins at the French doors and terminates in a shady pool of green at the far corner of the garden. The lines of the lawn swing the focus away from the garage to a large sycamore tree. The marked curvature of the lawn is further strengthened by a low brick wall that surrounds the semicircular sunken

patio adjacent to the conservatory. The shape is repeated in a low rosemary hedge that flanks the curving path.

The flowing lines of the path — made of tinted concrete — unite the different sections of the yard and echo the curving projections of the garage in one corner and the conservatory at the other end of the diagonal.

The garden's second level is created by a series of raised brick-walled beds, which have been

---

▼ **Design disguise** The flat, rectangular lot has lost its awkward shape through the addition of curving lines and changes in the levels of the beds and the patio.

filled with evergreen shrubs and trailers. The plants help to mask and soften the boundaries and large structures.

The third level consists of the sunken brick-paved patio. A generous space, three bricks lower than the lawn, it is perfect for entertaining and for viewing the rest of the garden.

Disguising an eyesore

What could have been an ugly intrusion — the corner garage — has been transformed into an attraction. The garage is built from weathered brick, and its most obvious feature — a long, blank wall — directly faces the conservatory and patio. Although the garage could not be totally hidden, its outline has been effectively obscured and softened.

The garage walls, embellished with brick piers, have become a decorative feature with the addition of Gothic-style windows and an ornamental lion's-head fountain and basin.

Water spouts from the lion's mouth and drops into a semicircular brick-faced basin. The bottom of the basin, which is hidden by clumps of euphorbias and a small-leaved hebe, is flanked by a pair of spindle-shaped conifers. At night the basin and the lion's head are lit from below.

Vertical brick piers link the garage facade with the concrete posts that support the wooden boundary fence. A single course of red bricks laid horizontally along the top of the garage wall also helps to unite the fence with the trelliswork at the rear of the garden.

The red brick pattern is repeated at the base of the garage walls, where it both enlivens and is broken up by the rounded shapes of perennials and annuals.

Viewed from the garden, the dark Gothic-style windows contrast pleasantly with the unadorned lighter brickwork. The play of light and shadow around this architectural feature is matched by the green variations in the planting plan.

Conservatory and patio

The large circular conservatory balances the effect of the garage and functions as a link between the house, patio, and garden. A pair of brick steps lead from the conservatory to the patio, which

Jutting out into the garden, the garage was a potential eyesore. It has been integrated into the garden and now makes a bold decorative feature. Bricks of a contrasting color, arched windows, and a fountain — all complemented by the planting — combine to break up the solid mass of the building.

A dark corner of the garden has been planted with a number of shade-tolerant shrubs, including *Fatsia japonica* and a dwarf tree ivy (x *Fatshedera lizei*). Periwinkle *(Vinca minor)* provides a good evergreen ground cover.

A lion's-head fountain, set against ornate brickwork, directly faces the patio and conservatory and creates a strong point of interest. Water spouts from the lion's mouth into a large basin, from which it is recirculated. Elegant euphorbias and a hebe mask the foot of the basin.

A stone owl keeps guard in a shady spot beneath a Norway maple (*Acer platanoides* 'Crimson King'). Shrubs, including mock orange and Japanese barberry, fill the corner. Nearby, a sandbox makes an attractive play area for young children.

An ornamental birdbath is framed by variegated ivies trained against the white house wall. The raised brick bed is planted with summer-flowering pink and white impatiens, white nicotiana, and trailing small-leaved ivy.

The semicircular sunken patio makes a perfect transition from the house to the garden, its curves echoed in the meandering concrete path. A thick hedge of rosemary provides a pleasant scent and blue flowers in early summer. Spotlights turn the area into an outdoor room at night and illuminate the steps to the lawn.

99

is paved with bricks in a basket-weave pattern.

The patio wall is broken by wide, shallow steps leading up to the lawn — spotlights illuminate these steps at night and show off the surrounding rosemary hedge. Facing west, the patio offers the best views of the sunset. A stone and metal barbecue is recessed into the patio wall.

The rosemary hedge provides a pleasant aromatic scent and blue flowers in summer. Despite its low height, it is dense and compact enough to provide a degree of seclusion — without hiding the rest of the garden. Regular clipping maintains its shape.

On the other side of the steps, following the curve of the patio, is a raised bed containing mixed herbs that repeat the rosemary theme and link the patio to the adjoining flower bed. The shrub roses and buddleia here partly conceal a small, triangular sunken sandbox.

▲ Clever disguise Lush planting beds draw the eye past the garage to the strong vertical of the Norway maple at the garden's rear. The success of this design trick — de-emphasizing the garage — depends on the owner's skill at integrating that structure into the landscape.

▼ Boundary markers A trellis-topped fence supports a sweet-scented honeysuckle and a repeat-flowering climbing rose. A glossy-leaved Mexican orange *(Choisya ternata)* and the silvery gray foliage of a groundsel *(Brachyglottis greyii)* further camouflage the wall.

Garden ornaments

Occasional stone pots, urns, and ornaments set around the garden are filled with a variety of foliage plants, summer bedding, and

bulbs. A stone owl, hidden in the shadows of a mature Norway maple, has become mossy with age and provides a surprise element — flanked by the scented white flowers of *Philadelphus* and the prickly stems and purple-green leaves of *Berberis thunbergii*, which turn a rich color in the fall.

The interplay between light and shade can also be seen in the stone birdbath by the house. The base of the pedestal is nestled in a small-leaved variegated ivy, while the birdbath itself is framed by a backdrop of a larger, darker-leaved variegated Algerian ivy (*Hedera canariensis* 'Gloire de Marengo'), which luxuriantly covers part of the white wall. Color contrast is provided by four blue-and-white tiles, decorated with flower and bird motifs, set higher on the wall.

Elsewhere in the garden — by the conservatory, on the patio, and close to the house — are several terra-cotta and stone containers. A wooden half barrel contains an evergreen camellia.

The planting scheme

A wide selection of easily maintained shrubs and shrubby perennials forms the backbone of the planting. The effect is one of a leafy perimeter of plants with different foliage colors and textures.

On the sheltered west side of the garden, a high wooden fence is partially covered with climbing *Hydrangea petiolaris* and blue-flowered ceanothus. Among other plants, the adjacent bed has red-leaved berberis, the dark green glossy leaves of sweetly scented Mexican orange (*Choisya ternata*), the light green leaves of flowering currant, and a small-leaved cotoneaster. These shrubs create a multitiered living covering that effectively disguises the tall fencing.

By the garage, in contrast, paler-leaved shrubs, such as a gray-leaved groundsel, have been used to brighten the facade and modify the dominating effect of a large expanse of brickwork. Ultrahardy white-flowered regal lilies *(Lilium regale)* and the white-flowered climbing common jasmine *(Jasminum officinale)* provide color. Exotic spurges, including *Euphorbia characias wulfenii* with its showy green-yellow flower heads, provide contrast with darker-leaved plants.

▲ **Wall features** Architectural touches — colored brickwork, Gothic-style arches, and a lion's-head fountain — turn a previously ugly feature into an attractive focal point. Evergreen planting at the foot of the wall and scrambling climbers above heighten the effect.

▶ **Brick buttresses** Large piers break up the garage wall, and climbing roses and common jasmine add to the disguise. The raised planting bed at the foot contains majestic white trumpet lilies and sprawling woolly-leaved lamb's ears *(Stachys byzantina)*.

▼ **Play corner** A sunken sandbox is set in a quiet corner close to the patio. Summer color comes from fragrant white-flowered mock orange *(Philadelphus)* and from an edging of garden pinks.

▲ **Ivy garland** Variegated Algerian ivy (*Hedera canariensis* 'Gloire de Marengo') covers the white house wall and frames an ornamental birdbath. In shade for much of the day, the raised bed is planted with impatiens, white nicotiana, and small-leaved trailing ivy.

◄ **Culinary herbs** A simple barbecue is recessed in the boundary wall of the patio. It is conveniently surrounded by a bed of fragrant herbs. Pink-flowered ceanothus and evergreen Japanese fatsia *(Fatsia japonica)* hide the wooden fence.

▶ **Impassive sentinel** A large moss-covered stone owl guards a shady corner of the garden from would-be intruders. *Berberis thunbergii* forms a spiny barrier, which is softened by mock orange and variegated ivies.

The green-yellow theme is reinforced by lady's-mantle *(Alchemilla mollis)*.

The garden has a strong spring planting scheme. Grape hyacinths *(Muscari aucheri)* and early hellebores *(Helleborus corsicus* and *H. foetidus)* are grouped beneath the water fountain.

Tulips have been planted under climbing and shrub roses. Three tulip cultivars provide bold splashes of color: the single early golden-orange 'General de Wet,' the midseason carmine-and-white 'Garden Party,' and the salmon-pink 'Clara Butt,' which flowers in late spring.

Blue-flowered spring anemones *(Anemone blanda* 'Atrocaerulea') are planted in a pair of urns stationed on either side of the French doors.

SHADY GARDENS

Large trees shut out light with their overhanging branches, but the problem is easily solved with shade-tolerant underplanting.

Dense shade can make a garden appealing in the heat of summer, but it also makes it impossible to grow many garden plants. Fortunately, there is a host of attractive, shade-tolerant plants from which to choose.

Many plants, especially shrubs, do well in varying degrees of shade. These are plants that naturally live in forest areas or in the dappled light of woodland clearings. They tend to have modest flowers but produce colorful berries, some of which may persist from late summer through the winter months. Many such shrubs do best on the slightly or markedly acid soil resulting from the buildup of rotted leaf debris.

The garden described here lies on slightly acid, moist soil. The soil has been improved over the years with doses of compost and mulches of shredded bark. The garden has been stocked with a wide variety of shrubs, many of Asian origin, such as aucubas.

The back of the house faces northwest, and the garden has an L shape. Apart from the extensive shaded area, other points of interest include a water garden, an adjacent area planted as a rock scree, and an attractive pergola surrounded by shrubs and climbers that require full sun.

Coping with shade

The long arm of this L-shaped garden is shaded for much of the day by the overhanging branches of several large yew trees. The lower branches of some of these have been lopped off, but there is dense shade over more than half of the garden, including the lawn. The immaculate condition of the lawn is due in part to the high quality of the original turf, made up of a shade-tolerant lawn seed mixture with a good proportion of fine fescue (*Festuca*). The lawn is fed in late spring and early fall with a granular turf fertilizer.

The lawn is the strong unifying feature. Its gently rippling form extends from a corner that lies in deep shade to the diagonally opposite, well-illuminated side. At the edge of the lawn are scalloped and straight-edged borders planted with a good mix of flowering shrubs, which help to disguise the straight lines of the perimeter

▼ **Moist shade** Many plants thrive in shade, provided the soil beneath is moist. Here, aucuba, cotoneaster, and fatsia make sizable mounds beneath large mature yew trees.

walls and the flagstones of the patio.

Plants for shade

At the foot of the garage wall, and edging the patio, is a bed with shrubs that do not object to the shade cast by the garden wall. The brightest spot is reserved for a golden-leaved form of common boxwood (*Buxus sempervirens* 'Aureo-variegata'). Its small leaves and slow growth contrast with a vigorous wall-grown *Pyracantha*, decked in summer with billowing white flower clusters and in fall with scarlet berries. The evergreen planting also includes a spring-flowering camellia, which thrives in the moist, acid soil.

The east-facing border, backed by a brick wall, is dominated by massive yew trees that cast permanent shade in spite of the removal of the lower branches. The sweeping curves of the lawn have created deeply undulating planting beds, in which the yews appear as integral parts of the design. Planted in the deepest shade are evergreen shrubs that can withstand such inhospitable sites — *Aucuba japonica*, which is easy to grow and tolerates air pollution, and the equally accommodating Japanese fatsia (*Fatsia japonica*), with its huge, glossy, deeply divided leaves.

Farther along the border, some shrubs are grouped to give a tiered effect, showing off various leaf forms, colors, and sizes. A low-growing cotoneaster (*Cotoneaster horizontalis*) is flanked by a Japanese maple (*Acer japonicum*) and *Skimmia japonica*. The cotoneaster has small pink flowers, succeeded by clusters of scarlet berries. Skimmias have fragrant creamy flowers and, if male and female plants are grown together, small, bright red berries. Their glossy, leathery green leaves contrast with the soft green foliage of the maple, which turns deep red by late summer. Shade-tolerant salmon-pink and white impatiens edge the curve.

In addition, a Mexican orange (*Choisya ternata*) benefits from this sheltered position. It bears white flowers with a scent of orange blossom in late spring.

An interesting corner

The main sweep of the lawn leads to a small circular pool, which is

Mature yew trees shade much of the garden for most of the day. However, their lower branches have been pruned off to allow some light to filter through, and shade-tolerant shrubs have been used extensively for underplanting. With their dark green foliage and red berries, the yews are attractive in their own right.

Shade-tolerant shrubs, many producing flowers and berries, fill the strongly curving border. *Aucuba japonica*, Japanese fatsia (*Fatsia japonica*), and low-growing *Cotoneaster horizontalis* provide a mix of leaf color, size, and form.

A circular pool is visible from every part of the garden and breaks up the curving sweep of the large lawn. Although in dappled shade from the trees, it catches the morning sun. A stone bench set against a back-drop of ornamental grasses and flowering shrubs makes a pleasant sitting area. Water playing from a small fountain provides a soothing note.

An alpine bed, built on builders' rubble and topped with quartz gravel and rocks, is tucked behind the pool. Dwarf conifers and mat-forming alpine plants dominate the planting, with alpine pinks and gentians for color accents.

Lawns can be a problem in a shaded garden. Here shade-tolerant turf with a high proportion of fine fescues (Festuca) is kept in good condition by feedings of slow-release organic turf fertilizers in late spring and early fall. The lawn's curved perimeter disguises the garden's rectangular shape.

A brick pergola on the sunnier side of the garden adds height to the overall design. It is covered in climbers, such as Kolomikta vine (Actinidia kolomikta), and climbing shrubs, including a California flannel bush (Fremontodendron californicum). Stone urns, under the pergola and on the patio, are filled with petunias and other bedding plants.

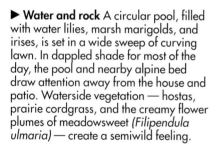

▲ **Pergola walk** A brick pergola roofed with wooden beams adjoins the sunny and sheltered patio. It is furnished with half-hardy climbers, hanging baskets, and urns planted with annual flowers.

▶ **Water and rock** A circular pool, filled with water lilies, marsh marigolds, and irises, is set in a wide sweep of curving lawn. In dappled shade for most of the day, the pool and nearby alpine bed draw attention away from the house and patio. Waterside vegetation — hostas, prairie cordgrass, and the creamy flower plumes of meadowsweet *(Filipendula ulmaria)* — create a semiwild feeling.

surrounded by a band of irregularly shaped flagstones. Wild European strawberry *(Fragaria vesca)* and other plants spill over the wide paving.

The pool is sited in dappled shade, and the harmonious and varied plants around it make this an especially pleasant, tranquil spot. The poolside planting includes clumps of hostas; feathery, plumelike flowers of meadowsweet *(Filipendula)*; and a cascade of green-and-white leaves of the variegated prairie cordgrass *(Spartina pectinata* 'Aureo-marginata'). Water irises, white water

lilies, and a white form of marsh marigold grow in the pool.

The pool is stocked with small koi carp and can be illuminated by a spotlight positioned below the water surface. A low fountain plays from a statue set into the center of the pool.

Behind the pool, hardy shield ferns *(Polystichum setiferum)* screen a second garden feature — a miniature alpine slope. This bed is atop some builders' rubble left on the site and thus is slightly above the general level of the garden. This material gives the bed the fast drainage necessary to

accommodate a range of alpine meadow plants.

The rubble has been topped with gray and pink quartz gravel, creating a light and colorful effect. For a natural look, rocks of different shapes and sizes jut out from the gravel mulch.

The plants chosen for the alpine area are tough and flourish with a minimum of care. They are mainly mat-forming plants of different shapes and colors, such as golden pearlwort *(Sagina subulata* 'Aurea') and a spectacular hybrid saxifrage that forms a silvery rosette, rather like a spider's web, with strap-shaped leaves and a very large, single white flower spike. Spots of color on the bed's graveled surface are provided by alpine pinks, summer-flowering gentians *(Gentiana septemfida)*, and clumps of fruiting alpine strawberries.

Dwarf conifers, with different shapes and foliage, add height to the alpine planting: crowded, vertically held golden green sprays of *Platycladus orientalis* 'Aureus Nanus' contrast well with the green-blue foliage of *Chamaecyparis lawsoniana* 'Minima Glauca.' A clump of bamboo, its grassy leaves arching above the wavy leaf rosettes of *Polygonum bistorta*, frames one side of the alpine area; at the back a young Japanese maple (*Acer palmatum* 'Dissectum') has finely cut green leaves that turn a glorious red in the fall.

The sunny side

From the French doors of the house, the view extends across the wide paved area that forms the patio and the pergola walk. The paving is a mixture of real flagstones and pavers cast to resemble them. At the end of the garden is another group of mature yew trees fronted by shrubs and herbaceous perennials and framed by the substantial brick pergola.

The pergola supports consist of

▶ **Wall climbers** Warm red bricks, irregularly laid, form a pleasing background for such half-hardy shrubs as *Pittosporum tenuifolium*, which is held in place on the pillar with wire. The color of the pale green and creamy white variegated leaves is picked up in a footing of white-flowered potentilla.

In a sheltered recess between the pillar and the fence, a Kolomikta vine shows off its tricolored foliage.

▼ **Idyllic retreat** In a peaceful corner bathed by the morning sun, a small stone seat by the pool matches the surrounding flagstone paving. The small statue, half hidden among lush vegetation, in turn conceals a softly playing water fountain.

PLANTS FOR SHADE

Aucuba japonica — evergreen shrub; white flowers; red berries.

Brunnera macrophylla 'Variegata' — perennial; green, white-splashed leaves; blue flowers.

Buxus sempervirens — evergreen shrub; green or variegated forms.

Convallaria majalis — perennial; rich green leaves; white flowers.

Digitalis grandiflora — perennial; green hairy leaves; creamy yellow flowers marked with brown.

Dryopteris dilatata — perennial fern; broad, arching fronds.

Euphorbia griffithii 'Fireglow' — perennial; medium green leaves; orange-red flowers.

Fatsia japonica — evergreen shrub; green leaves; white flowers in fall.

Gaultheria shallon — evergreen suckering shrub; leathery green leaves; pinkish-white flowers; purple berries.

Hedera helix cultivars — evergreen; dark green or variegated leaves.

Helleborus corsicus — evergreen perennial; grayish-green leaves; yellowish-green flowers.

Hosta fortunei 'Aureo-marginata' — moisture-loving perennial; yellow-green leaves; lilac flowers.

Hydrangea macrophylla — deciduous shrub; green leaves; pink, blue, or white flowers.

Hypericum calycinum — evergreen groundcover shrub; bright green leaves; yellow flowers.

Ilex crenata — evergreen holly; glossy dark green leaves; black berries if female plants are pollinated.

Iris foetidissima — dark green evergreen leaves; insignificant purple flowers; brilliant red seedpods.

Lamium maculatum 'Beacon Silver' — perennial; nettlelike silver-green leaves; pink flowers.

Ligustrum japonicum — evergreen privet; glossy dark green leaves; white flowers.

Mahonia aquifolium — evergreen shrub; dark green leaves, red-purple in fall; yellow flowers.

Saxifraga cortusifolia fortunei — perennial; green or purple-red leaves; white flowers.

Skimmia japonica — low evergreen shrub; white flowers; red berries if male and female plants are grown.

Vinca major — evergreen subshrub; blue-mauve flowers.

Vinca minor — evergreen groundcover; often variegated; white, blue, red, or purple flowers.

Viola cornuta 'Alba' — perennial groundcover; heart-shaped leaves; white flowers.

red bricks that match the external walls. At night a spotlight under the pergola roof illuminates the pale-flowered plants around and just beyond the pergola framework. The plants include a creamy white shrubby hydrangea (*Hydrangea arborescens* 'Grandiflora'), a white variegated form of shrubby dogwood (*Cornus alba* 'Elegantissima'), and at ground level, a white periwinkle (*Vinca minor* 'Alba').

Because the pergola receives the full afternoon sun, some half-hardy shrubs and climbers are able to do well in the sheltered recess formed between its pillars and the fence. The California flannel bush *(Fremontodendron californicum)*, a large-growing semievergreen shrub with handsome three-lobed leaves, bears stunning golden yellow flowers all through summer and fall. Here also grows the Kolomikta vine (*Actinidia kolomikta*), a slender climber outstanding for its leaf variegations of green, creamy white, and pink.

Twining around the pergola is a yellow-flowered winter jasmine and, for spring color, *Clematis montana rubens*. A variegated pittosporum grows up one pillar, merging with a white-flowered potentilla at ground level.

A hanging basket filled with brightly colored ivy-leaved geraniums gives a splash of summer color — a theme picked up by the bold-colored petunias planted in urns on the patio and by the white and salmon-pink impatiens at the front of the flower beds.

Keeping existing trees

The question of what to do with existing mature trees is important when you are redesigning a garden. Avid gardeners may be tempted to cut down large trees to allow more light for other plants, but it is worth thinking twice before asking an arborist to do this. Large trees bring an air of maturity to a newly designed garden and cannot be replaced in less than 15 to 20 years.

Rather than cut down a tree outright, consider carefully pruning off some of the larger branches to bring the tree to a suitable size and shape and to let more light and air into the garden.

The garden design here has incorporated the yew trees, whose dense shadows could have been a problem, and turned them into an asset. Yews, in spite of being poisonous in all their parts, are attractive for their evergreen foliage and their sprays of bright red berries.

▲ **Woodland sites** Moist, shady conditions are ideal for foliage plants such as hostas and many woodland ferns, including shield ferns *(Polystichum)*. Here, they mark the transition from the pool to a moist meadow.

▼ **Rocky bed** Simulating an alpine meadow, a moist rock- and gravel-covered bed seems a natural extension of the pool's stone-paved border. Creeping evergreens are planted among the rocks, with ferns and dwarf conifers to add height and provide foliage contrast.

Design for a purpose

Like houses, gardens become expressions of their owners' personalities or lifestyles, and as priorities change, so must they. Ideally, a garden should be planned to reflect the changing needs of the owners and have something to offer every member of the family. Children need space to play and areas to hide in, and if possible, a small bed or border where they can cultivate a garden of their own. Most adults want a place in which to relax or entertain and beds in which to grow plants and vegetables.

For some people, practical functions are less important, so the garden design may focus more exclusively on plant content. With a well-thought-out planting concept, it is not difficult to create a secluded garden where plants take priority, with shape, color, and texture becoming the deciding factors.

Sometimes physical or time constraints dictate that easy maintenance must outweigh all other considerations. In such cases the immaculate lawn yields to trouble-free paving, and plants that look after themselves replace time-consuming flower borders.

Illusion should be an integral part of any gardener's design tools. Visual tricks that fool the eye, such as a trellis that draws the eye to a nonexistent vanishing point or a mirror set into a wall to create the illusion of extra space where there is none, can help the gardener triumph over a site's physical limitations.

Play areas Family gardens, however small, should include spaces for children's activities.

GARDENS FOR CHILDREN

**A family garden should meet the
needs of all members, with space for youngsters
to play and adults to relax.**

Every parent knows the pleasure of being able to open the kitchen door and let boisterous children out in the yard. Whether the children spend an hour or a whole afternoon playing outside, the youngsters have a chance to exercise in the fresh air in a protected environment. (For safety's sake, all children need supervision even in their own backyard.)

On the other hand, very few parents are willing to sacrifice the whole garden to their children's pleasure. They are reluctant to allow it to become the outdoor equivalent of the playroom, full of toys and half-completed children's projects, with no peaceful or orderly haven for adults. Compromise is the best solution, and the results can be very attractive.

Design changes

Originally, this garden was a long, narrow, flat backyard — well maintained but lacking in character. Composed mainly of lawn, the south-facing yard had a path of irregular flagstones bordered by narrow flower beds. The path ran straight down the center of the yard to a shed at the far end, in the process cutting the yard into two narrow strips.

The layout was altered to meet the needs of a family with two small children: a low-maintenance garden based on a design that incorporated large, simple shapes and different levels.

The design includes a lawn and sitting area, a children's tricycle track, and a play area with a jungle gym. There is also a terrace and an outdoor dining area for entertaining, with privacy from neighboring houses and yards.

Although the garden is on the outskirts of a large town, the planting has a country feel,

rather than a sophisticated urban look. High priority is given to fruit trees, shrubs, and perennials — useful for flower arranging — as well as plants for year-round cover.

Creating a new garden

Circles form the basic geometry of the new layout. A wide, curving path connects the terrace, dining

area, and lawn with the shed and play area at the rear.

A strong diagonal axis is created by siting the circular lawn and dining area asymmetrically, so that the path has to curve first in one direction, then the other. This shape makes an ideal tricycle track and creates an illusion of additional width to the entire garden.

► **Circular themes** Clearly defined areas separate spaces for relaxation and for play. The patio, dining area, and lawn are surrounded by a curved tricycle track, which visually alters the narrow garden.

HANDS-ON GARDENING

◀ **Play and learn** Including children in your gardening work is a great way to introduce them to the wonders of nature. Just be sure to select activities suited to the child's physical skills and attention span. For example, filling a pot with soil is a task he or she can happily complete at an age as young as 18 months. With some thought you can find suitable gardening opportunities at every season.

▼ **Sunny day job** Even a toddler can sympathize with the plants' need for a "drink" and will be happy to oblige when the weather is warm. Gardening with children works best if you give them their own plot — a small raised bed is ideal. There they can experiment as they wish without disturbing your plantings.

The space between the circular shapes and the garden's outer edges becomes low raised beds, the extra topsoil coming from the excavation of the dining area. The flower beds are 6 in (15 cm) higher than the main garden level, and the dining area is sunk to a depth of about 1½ ft (45 cm). Drainage tile buried at the front of the beds carries off rainwater and snowmelt to a drain.

The play area is at the back of the garden and partly shielded by shrubs. Children can enjoy a feeling of secrecy, and the jungle gym, slide, and rough ground don't detract from the general appearance of the rest of the garden. The ground beneath the play equipment is covered with shredded bark, which provides a soft landing in case of falls. (Never rely on grass as a cushioning surface — it will soon give way to hard dirt.) The curving path becomes a natural extension of the play area.

Privacy from the neighboring houses is provided by sturdy trellises fixed to the top of the existing wooden fence along all the boundaries. Fruit trees, climbers, and rambling shrubs are trained against the fence.

Design alternatives

This garden design could also be based on more formal lines, with a generous-sized square or rectangular lawn and a similarly shaped dining area substituted for the circular one seen here.

In some ways, it would be an easier alternative. Laying bricks in circular or other curved patterns — especially in tight curves with a small radius — can involve extra work in cutting bricks to shape or having to vary the width of the mortar between bricks.

For a children's garden, however, curves are ideal. The service path that doubles as a children's track would be far less effective if it went at right angles around square lawn and dining areas. A straight path could cause young children to slip at sharp turns or tempt them to cut corners, resulting in bare dirt patches at the edges of the lawn.

You could, however, patch those corners with brick paving laid at a 45° angle to the path to allow for safe cycling and also break up the straight geometric lines of a rectangular layout.

In a design based on circular shapes, the depth of the borders along the perimeter varies widely. This adds more interest to the

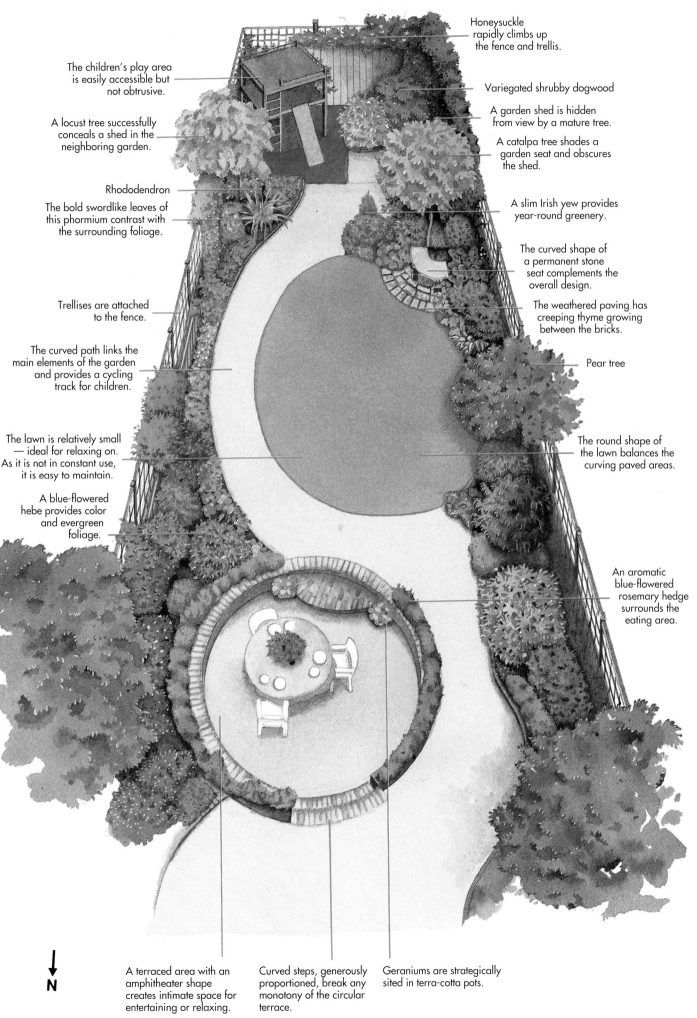

Honeysuckle rapidly climbs up the fence and trellis.

The children's play area is easily accessible but not obtrusive.

Variegated shrubby dogwood

A locust tree successfully conceals a shed in the neighboring garden.

A garden shed is hidden from view by a mature tree.

A catalpa tree shades a garden seat and obscures the shed.

Rhododendron

A slim Irish yew provides year-round greenery.

The bold swordlike leaves of this phormium contrast with the surrounding foliage.

The curved shape of a permanent stone seat complements the overall design.

Trellises are attached to the fence.

The weathered paving has creeping thyme growing between the bricks.

The curved path links the main elements of the garden and provides a cycling track for children.

Pear tree

The lawn is relatively small — ideal for relaxing on. As it is not in constant use, it is easy to maintain.

The round shape of the lawn balances the curving paved areas.

A blue-flowered hebe provides color and evergreen foliage.

An aromatic blue-flowered rosemary hedge surrounds the eating area.

↓
N

A terraced area with an amphitheater shape creates intimate space for entertaining or relaxing.

Curved steps, generously proportioned, break any monotony of the circular terrace.

Geraniums are strategically sited in terra-cotta pots.

HOUSE

113

planting and also serves to disguise the proportions of the garden. A layout based on rectangles would result in straight beds parallel with the path at the long boundaries and at right angles to it at the bottom and near the dining and patio area.

Future changes

The layout is designed to be flexible and easy to adapt when children's amenities are no longer needed. A vegetable garden, with a row of flowers for cutting, can eventually replace the play area. The spot is convenient as well as partially hidden from view. It could also accommodate a small greenhouse.

Although the rear part of the garden is slightly shaded by the end boundary fence, the area does get enough light for the normal range of flowers and vegetables. Some vegetables — for example,

lettuce, spinach, and radishes — appreciate protection from fierce summer sun.

A small water feature could be incorporated into the design at a later stage. (It is inadvisable to install even a small pool while toddlers are around.) Older children are fascinated by water and the wildlife it attracts — fish that dart about, birds that come to drink or chase insects, and frogs that mate and spawn.

Once the children grow older, ornamental pots may be set out in groups along the path. Filled with fuchsias, geraniums, or other bedding plants, they will add summer color without causing accidents or being knocked over.

The planting

As is often the case in urban gardens, the original acid soil was rocky and lacking in nutrients. It was improved by the addition of

commercially produced compost and slow-acting organic fertilizer. Leaves that fall in the garden each year are composted to continue this treatment.

The freestanding trees — a golden-leaved locust and a catalpa — were chosen for their moderate size and for their tolerance of air pollution. They will not grow too large for their allotted spaces. The flowering cherry (*Prunus subhirtella* 'Autumnalis') is another excellent small

---

▼ **Children's playground** A semisecret hideaway is set in one corner by a dense screen of tough shrubs and perennials. They include New Zealand flax (*Phormium tenax*), variegated shrubby dogwood (*Cornus alba* 'Elegantissima'), a columnar juniper, and bold *Euphorbia characias*. Honeysuckle covers the fence, and on the ground a thick layer of shredded bark will help cushion any falls.

tree for restricted spaces, producing its dainty white or pink flowers during mild spells in late fall and winter.

Along the fence are espaliered fruit trees, including pears, apples, peaches, and the sour Morello cherry, which grows well in a north-facing exposure. In limited spaces, it is advisable to plant self-fertile or compatible cultivars in order to be sure of getting a good crop when the young trees start to bear fruit.

Blackberries, which prefer a slightly acid soil, are also trained against the fence and tied in with wires. They are self-fertile thornless cultivars, and their lush foliage covers the wooden fence attractively.

Vitis coignetiae, an ornamental grapevine (also known as glory vine), clambers up the house. Its purple-black fruit is inedible, but the foliage turns bright crimson in fall.

A fragrant rosemary hedge is planted in the low wall around the dining area. Evergreen and long-lived (in mild, dry climates), rosemary tends to sprawl with age, but it responds well to pruning in the early spring.

The raised bed could also be used to contain a miniature herb garden with lemon balm, thyme, basil, purple-leaved sage, and marjoram. Rue and tansy are

▲ **House climbers** In a corner against the house, two vigorous climbers enjoy each other's company. They take up little ground space but quickly cover the sunny upright support with leafy stems and purple clematis flowers and the long orange-red tubes of the Chilean glory flower *(Eccremocarpus scaber)*. Outside the Deep South, the latter must be grown as an annual.

◀ **Centerpiece** Beneath the handsome canopy of a catalpa *(Catalpa bignonioides)*, a curved bench repeats the circular design of the garden. Creeping thyme grows among the cracks and lady's-mantle *(Alchemilla mollis)* droops its green flowers over the edges. Set on well-weathered bricks, the view is toward the ornamental part of the garden.

strongly aromatic, but some find their scents unpleasant.

There is a roughly equal balance of evergreen and deciduous plants, so the garden has appeal even in winter. Ivy, escallonia, elaeagnus, evergreen climbing honeysuckle (*Lonicera japonica*), *Viburnum davidii*, privet, hebe, and several dwarf junipers provide a year-round backdrop for various herbaceous perennials, deciduous shrubs and climbers, and several espaliered fruit trees.

Children in the garden

Planting has largely been confined to the boundary borders, leaving the center open for play. The lawn is a hard-wearing seed mixture that stands up to boisterous games; it can be planted with naturalized bulbs after the children are grown up.

While children are young, it is sensible to stick to tough plants and to avoid any with spiky or spiny leaves and stems. Several garden plants, including labur-

▲ **Family garden** Mature trees and evergreen foliage plants in this small urban garden create a sense of privacy as well as secret hiding places for young children.

num, lily of the valley, and yew berries, are poisonous and should not be planted. If possible, give your children their own little garden (see box, page 112) to nurture their knowledge and appreciation of plants and gardening.

CREATIVE PLANT DESIGNS

Imaginative use of foliage plants can transform the most modest backyard into a miniature haven of tranquillity.

Planning and planting a very small landscape are often more difficult than creating a garden on a large lot. If a garden is small, the whole can be taken in at a glance, which is quite a challenge at the planning stage.

Without a large lawn, curving flower borders, or the lure of hidden areas glimpsed through a hedge or trees, interest must be created by the skillful use of plants and materials. Attention to detail is vital here — every plant or stone counts.

This tiny garden is an excellent example of small-scale planning. Level and almost square in shape, it is situated behind the house and faces south. Bounded by tall fences, the garden is too small for a lawn to make much sense. Instead, it is planned as an easily maintained area of pavement, with borders roomy enough for a good selection of plants.

The accent is on raised beds, a central platform, and plants with strong foliage shapes, textures, and colors, though some plants also have attractive flowers.

Many shrubs are evergreen, and gray or silver foliage plays an important role. Several perennials keep their foliage all year, so the garden has a well-furnished look in winter.

The flower colors are soft and restful — bright hues could be overpowering in so small a space.

▼ **Dramatic centerpiece** The raised borders here are filled with foliage plants, while the platform of pavement in the center is stocked with sprawling alpines. The effect is of green walls enclosing a stage carpeted with silver.

And as the garden is sunny, colors from the cool rather than the warm part of the spectrum are used to avoid a garish effect.

A mellow, grayish stone is used for the paving. As no two slabs are identical in size or tone, there is no hint of geometric monotony.

As a dramatic note, a raised area of pavement is set at the garden's center to serve as a stage for choice plant specimens. On one side of this is another bed, built on a slightly higher level.

The straight-edged boundary borders are also raised above the level of the garden floor. Because these beds occupy a small area, it was easy to supplement their impoverished soil with fresh loam topsoil.

The raised features give the impression that the paving is a sunken part of the garden — an excellent way of introducing variety to the small, square shape. Another benefit is that the raised plants, particularly the smaller types, can be better appreciated.

All through the garden, the selection of plants and their placement soften the hard edges of the masonry, with plants billowing forward or arching down.

Foliage centerpiece

Plants grown in paving look extremely effective, but in a very small space greenery spilling everywhere may restrict movement. Here, on a raised platform, plants are displayed to advantage without getting in the way.

The varying shapes, textures, and colors of plant foliage in the central bed provide interest during much of the year. Some of the plants offer the additional advantage of seasonal flowers.

The dark green column of an Irish yew (*Taxus baccata* 'Fastigiata') placed near one corner makes a good vertical contrast to the low paving and sets off the lighter shades of the other actors on this stage. Its near neighbors are dwarf yellow-flowered sisyrinchiums and carpeting gray rosettes of *Antennaria parvifolia*.

The plants in this raised paved area have interesting foliage. The soft, gray-leaved semihardy trailer *Helichrysum petiolatum* accompanies the tender *Echeveria secunda glauca,* with succulent blue-gray rosettes. Other sources of attractive foliage include the blue-gray leaves of the sprawling

A good view from the house — both from the ground floor and the upper stories — was an important design consideration. Exotic half-hardy plants thrive in the shelter of the house wall.

Delicate shapes and colors of flowers and foliage work best in a small, sunny space where there is no lush green lawn nearby to temper the brighter shades. Light colors give a feeling of open space.

Plants in pots are moved periodically, either to display flowers or to give the plants extra light or shelter. This adds flexibility to the design, as even a slight change in arrangement can make a tiny garden look quite different.

A sense of seclusion — this garden's greatest attraction — is provided by climbers and shrubs at the boundaries. All have slender, open growth patterns, which help to avoid a junglelike effect.

The mellow paving, quiet in both hue and texture, creates a restful mood. A central platform with raised beds at the boundaries enhances the feeling of seclusion.

Changes of level add interest to this garden's small, square shape. Raised beds are ideal for bringing low-growing rock garden plants closer to eye level.

N

Euphorbia myrsinites and the white-backed leaves of pink-flowered annual gazanias.

The central planting stage is raised to a higher level at one end, creating a bed for shrubs chosen for their foliage colors. The difference in levels adds welcome height and overcomes the problem of a flat-looking focal point. As the shrubs reach maturity, they are pruned to shape or removed entirely to make room for different plants, thus giving scope for new foliage and color combinations.

The swordlike leaves of a purple-leaved variety of New Zealand flax *(Phormium tenax)* rise as an

▶ **Boundary cover** With its roots firmly anchored in shady soil, the vigorous *Clematis* 'Comtesse de Bouchaud' clothes the trellis-topped fence with a mass of rose-pink, golden-eyed blooms through the summer, enthusiastically partnering a perennial pea.

◀ **Foliage contrast** A sunny house wall shelters the silver-gray filigree leaves of a semievergreen *Artemisia arborescens*. With protection from winter cold, this shrubby perennial has grown to treelike proportions to contrast well with the imposing white-and-purple flower spikes of bear's-breeches *(Acanthus mollis)*.

emphatic vertical feature in this bed. A stronger purple comes from the leaves of a plum-colored smoke tree *(Cotinus coggygria* 'Royal Purple'), contrasting with the soft silver-gray of a shrubby senecio beside it.

More purple foliage, from *Berberis thunbergii* 'Atropurpurea Nana,' is backed by the striped leaves of gardener's-garters *(Phalaris arundinacea* 'Picta'). The color scheme is repeated in the raised border with the orange-red flowers of *Lilium* 'Enchantment' and Peruvian lilies *(Alstroemeria ligtu* hybrids).

Boundaries and borders

The boundaries of this secluded garden are thickly clothed with deciduous climbers and shrubs to mask the fence and to give agreeable views across the garden.

Climbers are strongly represented here, including the large-flowered *Clematis* 'Comtesse de Bouchaud,' whose golden-centered, rose-pink blossoms are charmingly associated with the

white perennial pea (*Lathyrus latifolius* 'White Pearl').

The large pure white flowers of *Clematis* 'Marie Boisselot' are particularly noticeable at dusk. A large-leaved glory vine *(Vitis coignetiae)* fills much space and produces colorful fall foliage.

Amid the border shrubs is the butterfly bush (*Buddleia davidii* 'Alba'), whose long, arching white plumes contrast with the rather flat, pinkish lace-cap heads of a tall *Hydrangea aspera sargentiana*. The glossy green, gold-variegated leaves of *Elaeagnus pungens* 'Maculata' as well as the white-splashed foliage of the dogwood *Cornus alba* 'Elegantissima' light up darker corners.

▲ **Planting pockets** Gaps in the raised platform bed are planted with low-growing foliage plants. Purple-leaved bugle (*Ajuga reptans* 'Atropurpurea') creeps along the cracks, mingling with gray-leaved trailing *Helichrysum petiolatum* and the silvery blue leaf rosettes of echeverias. An Irish yew stands like a green punctuation mark in one corner, with color from pink gazanias and yellow evening primroses.

▲ **Sunbather** The evergreen houseleek *(Sempervivum montanum)* creeps slowly along to form low carpets of dark green leaf rosettes studded in summer with short, stout stems of purple-pink flowers. It flourishes in full sun and any well-drained soil.

▼ **Leafy retreat** The mellow tones of paving and raised garden beds blend effectively with a wealth of foliage colors and textures. Subdued flower shades avoid any jarring note in the exuberant leaf cover and add a soft glow when dusk falls.

▲ **Purple and silver** Strong leaf colors serve to highlight each other. The centerpiece in this dramatic grouping is an erect clump of purple-variegated *Phormium tenax,* which rises above the near-circular leaves of *Cotinus coggygria* 'Royal Purple.' Fine contrast in texture, shape, and color comes from gray-green senecios and striped gardener's-garters, fronted by silvery-leaved *Convolvulus cneorum.*

In less sunny spots are shade-tolerant perennials, including such foliage plants as *Helleborus corsicus, Astrantia major,* the variegated *Hosta undulata* 'Uni-vittata,' as well as golden-flowered *Rudbeckia fulgida* and sweet-scented nicotiana.

In sunny spots, semishrubby *Euphorbia characias wulfenii,* silvery artemisias, and woolly-leaved lamb's ears thrive.

Another feature of the garden is the careful placement of a few well-chosen pots. Their rounded shapes contrast with the straight lines of the paving, and the choice of plants complements the design. Silvery gray artemisia foliage looks lovely against its terra-cotta container.

LOW-MAINTENANCE GARDENS

Conifers and evergreen and deciduous shrubs need little attention but furnish a garden with color and interest throughout the year.

The garden described here has acquired a mature look in less than 5 years, mainly because a good selection of permanent plants in the form of trees and shrubs was made at the outset.

The small suburban garden, rectangular in shape and with acid soil, was planned for low maintenance and year-round interest. Weathered bricks, laid in a herringbone pattern, have replaced the traditional lawn area. A lawn would have worked just as well in this particular planting scheme, but it does require mowing and edging. Moreover, in a small garden, it usually needs fairly frequent aeration and fertilization to compensate for constant wear.

The pavement of light-colored bricks provides a plain setting, ideal for showing off the plants. The intricate shapes and textures of the leaves can be appreciated against the uncluttered, flat surface. Low retaining walls are made of the same bricks as those used for paving, giving the garden coherence. Bricks installed in an intricate pattern can be costly and time-consuming to install. A similar effect can be achieved using concrete pavers; these are interlocking units that are easier and less costly to install.

The curved shape of the paved area disguises the lot's conventional rectangular shape and gives the garden immediate interest. The addition of a circular island bed, set off-center, helps to break up the basic shape even more and prevents the eye from taking in the whole garden at once. It also does much to soften the effect of a large expanse of hard surface.

For a softer effect, small, prostrate, mound-forming plants can be squeezed into crevices between the bricks, or some bricks can be removed to make room for "creepers" such as *Arabis*, saxifrages, and thyme. Other rock plants with showy flowers, such as *Campanula, Dianthus,* and *Raoulia,* would break up the rigid appearance of the rectangular brick paving even more.

▼ **Paved flooring** Brick forms a pleasing background for evergreen foliage. Prostrate shrubs, such as *Cedrus libani* 'Nana,' creeping junipers, boxwood, and *Euonymus fortunei* 'Emerald 'n' Gold,' minimize weed growth.

Designing with evergreens

In this garden the planting relies heavily on conifers — mostly junipers and cypresses. They have been used with definite style to provide basic substance and form. Some taller specimens have been planted around the edges to give the boundary a more interesting shape, as well as to create privacy and shelter.

The two prominent Monterey cypresses (*Cupressus macrocarpa*) are fast-growing species that quickly become a good hedge or windbreak. Their bright yellow foliage and strong upright shapes are offset by a columnar Oriental arborvitae (*Platycladus orientalis*), which assumes a more rounded outline with age.

To add to the variety of shapes and tones of green, there is a Lawson cypress (*Chamaecyparis lawsoniana*) near the house. Its drooping sprays of rich green, aromatic foliage take on a beautiful reddish glow in spring from a profusion of crimson catkins.

Completing the picture, the rear boundary is marked by the conical outline of a group of junipers. They are dark green and have small, dark berrylike cones.

Coniferous trees come into their own in winter. Their great advantage is that, unlike deciduous trees, they retain their leaves throughout the coldest months, always look good, and can be appreciated year-round.

When coniferous trees are planted in groups, as they are here, their great diversity of texture, form, shape, and color is most effectively displayed. A strong conifer planting is particularly noticeable if it is either intermixed with some deciduous trees and shrubs or used as a dominant background for them.

The characteristics of the two groups of trees — coniferous and deciduous — complement each other and have been used effectively here. At the rear of the garden, a mature whitebeam (*Sorbus aria*) screens out the neighbors' yard. Few trees can surpass the beauty of the whitebeam in fall, when its leaves turn russet and gold and its huge clusters of berries deepen to crimson.

Halfway along the western boundary, a purple-leaved cherry plum (*Prunus cerasifera* 'Atropurpurea') also creates privacy and offers continuous pleasure

▲ **Green boundaries** This small, easily managed garden has an architectural design — its form and outline are the dominant elements. Curving beds and borders obscure the actual shape; changes in surface levels and plant heights give an illusion of space and depth.

◄ **Carefree shrubs** A curved bed close to the patio is planted with evergreen shrubs that largely look after themselves. Azaleas maintain their glossy foliage year-round and burst into vivid bloom in late spring. Creeping junipers and trailing ivy nearly eliminate the need for weeding, and honeysuckle covers the boundary fence.

from early spring, when it is covered in a mass of pink-budded white flowers and the young, dark red leaves mature to deep purple.

Dwarf and slow-growing conifers have been used in conjunction with the tree and shrub elements of the planting. They are an asset for their shape and texture alone. For example, *Thuja occidentalis* 'Rheingold,' a slow-growing specimen that will eventually reach a height of only 10 ft (3 m), has a broadly conical outline and amber-gold foliage that is especially distinctive in winter. It contrasts boldly with the rich green conifers and other plants, such as the hebes and junipers behind it.

Some trees, such as the willow *(Salix)* in the island bed and the boxwood *(Buxus sempervirens),*

have been heavily clipped into rounded topiary shapes in order to give the garden a more formal feeling.

Ground cover

Plenty of prostrate, mat-forming species of conifers, such as *Juniperus horizontalis, Cedrus libani* 'Nana,' and the deciduous red-berried *Cotoneaster horizontalis,* have been used to cover the soil and create a thick, lush effect at ground level. They are spaced out around the borders, near the house, and in the farthest corners of the garden so that it never looks bare, not even in the depths of winter.

The shrub border

Shrubs are, above all, practical plants. Once settled, they look after themselves, needing only a

little training and pruning to keep them shapely, healthy, and in bounds. Yet when choosing them, you must be patient — the most handsome types take time to mature. A period of 5 years or more after planting a shrub border is required before the infant, individual bushes crowd together to make a fully grown garden. In the meantime, short-lived perennials or annuals and bedding plants can be used to fill the gaps.

However, there are some "instant" shrubs that grow to almost full size in a mere 2 or 3 years, and several of these, such as rockroses, buddleia, and ceanothus, are used here to give the appearance of maturity. These vigorous shrubs usually bear a profusion of flowers and root easily from cuttings. Flowering currants, mock oranges, and almost all willows fall into the same useful category of quick-growing shrubs.

Seasonal value

One of the most reliable and important contributions that shrubs make to a garden is their combination of flowers, leaves, and highly colored fruit, each displayed at a different time of year. The shrubs here have been carefully chosen to provide a year-round show. The garden is in a continuous state of development, one shrub coming into bloom as another one fades.

The flowering season starts in midspring, when the gracefully arching stems of the evergreen *Berberis darwinii* flare into a vivid orange flower display and the azaleas come into blossom. These have been purposefully planted near the house, where they can be best appreciated.

Farther back, toward the rear of the garden, small white urn-shaped flowers are carried in drooping clusters on the glossy-leaved *Pieris japonica.* The deep green background of conifers makes these flowers seem like sparkling jewels. The shapely *Genista lydia* forms a mound of

◀ **Ground-cover plants** The vigorous *Hypericum calycinum* grows quickly to form a solid carpet that glows with golden yellow flowers over many months. Flowering dead nettle spreads just as quickly, and its variegated leaves contrast pleasingly with prostrate juniper and small-leaved ivy.

scene where all plant types shelter and complement each other.

Interspersed among the shrubs are the long, swordlike leaves of irises, and in the island bed, the slender forms of lilies and ornamental grasses complement the bushy habits of evergreen shrubs. Bulbs are at home under low ground cover, and in spring the snowdrops, winter aconites, and daffodils look spectacular bursting through the mats of ivy.

Small clumps of annuals and bedding plants — mainly pinks, nicotianas, and geraniums — add color and texture to the varied evergreens in the borders. Hanging baskets near the house and strategically placed pots provide seasonal color.

◄ **Foliage colors** A small rock garden displays a range of evergreen leaf colors. The pale leaves of yellow-flowered creeping Jenny (*Lysimachia nummularia* 'Aurea') blend with the variegated foliage of *Euonymus fortunei* and the reddish *Epimedium* x *rubrum*.

piercing yellow in spring. Some other early-flowering shrubs that would create a similar effect at this time of year are flowering quinces, flowering currants, mahonias, and daphnes.

The structurally handsome *Cornus controversa* blooms in late spring and early summer and then produces interesting blue-black berries in autumn, at the same time as the leaves turn purple-red before falling. The hebes reach the peak of their long flowering season in late summer, as do the fuchsias and the buddleias.

The evergreen *Elaeagnus pungens* 'Maculata' is a large, robust shrub that assumes importance during late fall and winter. It bears silvery flowers in late fall, and its big, dark green, silver-backed leaves are each marked with a bold golden splash.

In addition to being used as a backdrop, the shrubs have been integrated with other plants. Herbaceous perennials, bulbs, and annuals have been planted between the main masses and treated as equal partners in a

▶ **Island bed** A grafted pussy willow (*Salix caprea* 'Pendula') is the focal point in this bed. Its drooping silvery and gold catkins look stunning in late winter.

Vigorous late-summer-flowering buddleias fill one corner, their flower plumes bright against conifers.

Hardy, deep red fuchsia flowers add dashes of welcome color.

N

Sculptural junipers provide a plain dark green foil for mixed shrubs and annuals.

A tall golden conifer screens out the neighbors' yards.

Scented evergreens, such as lavender, grow quickly to fill out borders.

The black-purple leaves of a cherry plum provide light shade in summer.

A spindle tree (Euonymus japonica) fills a gap between conifers to create a hedge.

Clumps of irises add an early-flowering vertical element among young shrubs.

The gold-green leaves of Elaeagnus pungens 'Maculata' contrast with the dark juniper foliage.

A clipped willow and boxwood create a formal island bed.

A trellis at the boundary supports climbing plants.

Quick-growing 'Goldheart' ivy hides the fence with year-round cover.

Spectacular and welcome spring color comes from azaleas and Berberis darwinii.

The gentle curves of the borders distract the eye from the actual shape of the lot.

Long-lasting red-hot pokers (Kniphofia) make a colorful focal point in the island bed.

Sweet-scented, mauve-flowered Wisteria sinensis decorates the pergola.

A rambling 'Albertine' rose rapidly covers the pergola.

The low-maintenance brick pavement has been laid in a herringbone pattern.

Sweet Williams self-seed to provide bold splashes of pink in summer.

HOUSE

127

▲ **Scented canopy** A wooden pergola extending across the sunken patio will in time be completely covered by wisteria on one side and the rambling 'Albertine' rose on the other. Meanwhile, hanging baskets of bedding plants provide seasonal color.

From the patio the neighboring gardens are screened out by dense boundary planting, and the curving lines of the design invite closer inspection of specimens in the far corners.

▶ **Space fillers** A young yellow-leaved mock orange (*Philadelphus coronarius* 'Aureus') in the foreground is nursed along in a gap in the mixed border, sheltered by the leaves of a hydrangea. When it has put on more growth, it will be moved to a permanent site, where it can reach its ultimate size of 8 ft (2.4 m) and put on a proper display of its fragrant creamy white flowers.

TROMPE L'OEIL

A number of tricks that create believable illusions of space or suggest hidden secrets can be used successfully in the smallest of gardens.

The French expression *trompe l'oeil* means "deceives the eye." Here, it refers to the creation of illusions that make a garden appear larger or more interesting than it is, add an element of beauty, or play a lighthearted joke.

"Forcing the perspective" is an example of this sort of optical illusion, and it is often used to give a feeling of greater depth to a small garden. Often a garden is out of scale with the house; if the house is grand in style but set on an ordinary-size lot, the garden may seem meager. To give an illusion of greater depth to a short yard, a designer may run a broad garden path from a back door or window straight back to the rear property line. Instead of keeping the sides of the path parallel, however, the designer subtly alters the angles so that they run gradually toward each other. As the path grows narrower, it seems to recede into the distance, making it seem much longer than it actually is.

This illusion can be reinforced by edging the path with hedges that are clipped shorter and narrower the farther they are from the house — in effect, the hedges seem to recede into the distance as well. Similarly, a fence that diminishes in size as it runs away from the house creates an illusion of distance.

The simplest trick for creating an illusion of depth is to plant full-size shrubs and trees next to the house and landscape the rear of the garden with dwarfs.

These same tricks can be reversed to make a garden seem shallower than it is, but that is rarely desirable.

Other deceptions

Concealing the boundaries of a small garden makes it seem bigger: dense shrubbery around the perimeter is the most effective solution. Breaking up the space, however small, is also an effective visual trick. Trellises, hedges, narrow beds, or broad shrubberies that extend into the central area of a garden, for example, encourage the eye to imagine that the space beyond extends farther and wider than it really does.

Altering the symmetry of a garden can make it seem more spacious — for example, allowing a path to curve gently rather than proceed in a straight line. If a straight line is wanted, put it to one side of the garden rather than straight down the middle.

Mirrors

More than any other object, mirrors create an illusion of space in a confined area, doubling whatever image they reflect. The corner of a garden, especially where the two legs of an L-shaped garden meet, is suitable for such a trick. Site the mirror so that the junction appears to offer a choice of

◀ **Wall mural** Summer appears to linger in this elaborate trompe l'oeil painting. A false arch depicts a lush garden forever green, in contrast to the real garden in its late fall mood.

paths, one the real leg, the other its reflection. A blank wall is another possible location or immediately behind a feature, such as a statue or pool.

Setting a mirror at an angle to the viewer is usually more effective than setting it directly in front, because as soon as you can see your own reflection approaching, the illusion of additional space is destroyed.

As well as being angled to reflect another part of the garden, a mirror should reflect a light, bright image rather than a dark one — a bit of sky, for example, or a sun-filled border.

A broad, unbroken expanse of mirror is less convincing than one that is slightly obscured. A flat

trellis backed by a mirror makes a good combination, especially if some climbers are encouraged to grow around it. Placing a mirror immediately behind a gate or a door- or window-shaped frame also helps the eye accept the trick, giving the illusion of space beyond. Even more effective is a mirror behind a three-dimensional trellis or ironwork arch, creating an enticing tunnel that the eye, if not the body, is invited to explore.

With a semicircular pool backing onto a wall, use a carefully placed mirror on the wall to complete the circle, doubling the size visually. To make a pool seem to be recessed, place a mirror a little below ground level and mask it

slightly with foliage; by reflecting the sky above, it would give the illusion of a recessed pool.

Do not, however, make the mistake of using too many mirrors. An infinitely receding tunnel of images created by reflecting one mirror within another quickly loses its amusement value. Indeed, multiple mirrors reproduce reflections so many times that they give a garden a peculiarly crowded feeling rather than a sense of increased space.

Outdoor mirrors, even more than those in bathrooms, are vulnerable to changes in temperature as well as humidity. Tell your supplier that the mirror is to be installed outdoors. It must be heavy-duty, at least ¼ in (6 mm)

▲ **Water sport** A roof garden, turned into a secluded, leafy pool, seems to have attracted a passing bird. A fountain sprays water at the sculpture's feet, realistically simulating the moment of impact, while hiding the bird's base.

▲ ▶ **False perspective** Specially constructed trelliswork gives the impression of a pergola. Twining sprays of foliage and pots of flowering plants, arranged at the base of the trellis, add credibility to the deception.

▶ **Conjuring trick** Plants clamber up panels of ordinary trellising in front of a wall. In the center, cleverly distorted trellising draws the eye into the illusion of an arch; a tiny statue and ramp painted like receding brickwork complete the trick.

131

▲ Tricks of the trade Huge urns vanish into a stylized background. Although the painting does not try to trick the eye, a grouping of real urns in front of it reinforces the three-dimensional impression of movement out of the picture and toward the viewer.

thick, with the back protected against corrosion. A mirror that is sheltered from drips by overhanging roof eaves, wall coping, or a trellis is likely to last longer than one completely exposed to the elements. Lastly, a mirror is helpful only when clean, so allow reasonable access to it.

Murals

Painting leafy scenes, landscapes, or lofty architecture to create an airy perspective in a confined space is a form of trompe l'oeil that goes back at least to ancient Rome. As a refuge from the intense heat of the Mediterranean summer, Livia, the wife of Augustus Caesar, had a cool underground barrel-vaulted room built.

The inside was painted to look like a beautiful balustraded garden, complete with ornamental trees, shrubs, flowers, and even birds. In Roman town houses, courtyards had frescoes depicting trees and flowers to give an increased sense of space.

In today's urban and suburban gardens, basement areas or overshadowed spots can be decorated with realistic or imaginative landscapes planted as sparsely or as densely as taste and budget allow.

Decide at the outset whether the mural should be flat and simplified, in the manner of a stencil, or three-dimensional, which involves perspective, a vanishing point, and shadows. Flat images are decorative but may be less

▶ Mirror images A tiny sunken garden appears twice its size after a huge mirror has been attached to a white wall. The trellis and climbing clematis help the illusion. Mirrors work best when they reflect still scenes — movement tends to destroy the illusion.

effective as visual tricks. Three-dimensional images, such as a building, an avenue of trees, or balustrades receding into the distance, are more difficult to do well but are often more effective at creating a feeling of depth and spaciousness. Consider hiring a professional artist, since a poorly executed design is far worse than a straightforward wall painted white.

As with mirrors, murals are especially effective on end walls, which otherwise define the limits of a garden. Blank walls opposite windows or French doors overlooking the garden are also suitable and can be enjoyed indoors and out. It isn't necessary to paint the entire wall: a trompe l'oeil "window" in a wall, giving a painted view of a pool with a bubbling fountain or of rolling countryside with tree-lined avenues "beyond," can be delightful.

Consult a professional artist about the type of paint suitable for an external mural; it is usually necessary to waterproof and

---

▶ **Illusions of space** A mirrored archway creates an impression of an inviting garden beyond the conifer screen. Made from a single sheet of tough glass, the mirror needs frequent cleaning to maintain the illusion.

prime the wall before applying the image.

Trellises

You can buy an arched wooden wall-mounted trellis with a built-in false perspective — a central eye-level vanishing point toward which the upper battens radiate. Such a trellis is more effective hung against a plain or stuccoed wall than a brick one, whose own parallel and right-angled lines destroy the illusion. And though some softening effect from foliage and flowers is desirable, heavy, lush growth tends to obscure the deception of the trellis. Setting a mirror at the trellis's center completes the illusion.

Regular maintenance is necessary, especially in the case of wooden trellising, which must be repainted or stained periodically. Be sure to choose fast-growing climbing plants to train over the trellis so that they reestablish themselves promptly after being cut away to permit painting.

Sculpture

There are many ways of using sculpture as trompe l'oeil; all require a firm foundation and mounting for the statue to stay upright and secure. Most also require a large amount of time and money, since trompe l'oeil statuary is not mass produced.

Before embarking on such a project, remember that a witty sculpture could lose its charm if you are endlessly exposed to it. Ideally, you should store the sculpture and take a break from the joke from time to time.

You can treat the garden as a front-facing stage and build "flats" — wooden, marine-grade plywood, or chipboard cutouts painted to look three-dimensional and supported from behind with wooden struts, as on film sets. Suitable subjects might be classical stone statues, columns, ruins, or animals such as a grazing horse or even a flock of geese.

The drawback is fairly obvious: as with a front-facing stage, the trick only works when viewed straight on; a sideways view exposes the object as a cut-out fake. It is best to site flats at the very end of a garden and to back the "statue" with shrubs or other plants to help conceal the supporting framework.

Three-dimensional statues that pretend to look real — life-size and realistically painted fiberglass or plastic sheep, for example — take the trompe l'oeil one stage further. On a smaller scale a gray stone cat could forever perch in a tree or on a roof, or a bronze water bird could be always landing on the surface of a pool, with perhaps a small fountain spray of water to simulate the moment of landing.

Color

Painting a wall in pale colors or white gives the impression that the wall is closer than it is. Painting the same wall with dark colors makes it seem farther away. White, black, or any other color will also alter the visual impression of an area. In a long, narrow garden, for example, planting a white border at the far end will make it seem closer to the viewer; in a short, wide garden, planting the end bed with dark-colored flowers has the opposite effect, pushing it back visually.

A post or trellis on a wall — even a change in the material the wall is made of — will interrupt the eye, giving the impression of a smaller plane. By painting everything in a single color — including the interruptions — it's possible to "stretch" the surface.

If the garden is truly postage-stamp size, however, these tricks of color will not be effective. In such a case it would be best to use mirrors or murals.

◀ **Trick upon trick** A symmetrical trellis on a wall draws the eye inward to its vanishing point — a mirror reflection of another trellis opposite. The illusion is completed with trick planting — plastic holly adorns the arches in the trellis.

Theme gardens

Certain situations call for particular designs. Garden size, surrounding landscape, soil type, time, and many other factors place constraints on a design, but these need not be overly restricting. Roof gardens, for example, are unalterable in size, demand shelter from the sun, and require wind-resistant plants. But within these limitations and those posed by the load-bearing capacity of the roof itself, there are numerous options for creating miniature landscapes among the clouds.

In the sunny Southwest, the designer may envisage a formal garden surrounded by whitewashed walls and filled with earthy colors reminiscent of the Mediterranean regions of southern Europe. Shade, on the other hand, need not be a barrier to good garden design. Shady sites suit many layouts, from informal arrangements of woodland plants to water gardens of Oriental splendor and formal designs that include topiary, clipped hedges, and geometric stone features.

An alpine landscape can be created on a rocky site, with the help of exquisite dwarf conifers and compact high-mountain plants with brilliantly colored flowers. Such sites also lend themselves to traditional Japanese gardens, elegantly informal compositions that seem to capture the essence of nature itself. Rocks and water are the inspiration for these gardens, in which trees and shrubs are chosen for their form and color to add depth and perspective to small spaces.

On top of the world Wind-resistant shrubs and climbers transform a rooftop garden into a sheltered oasis.

ROOF AND TERRACE GARDENS

**Upper-story gardens, furnished
with tough, wind-resistant plants, make ideal outdoor
rooms for relaxation and entertaining.**

A roof or terrace garden may serve as an addition to a ground-level garden or, in the case of apartment dwellers, the only available space. Although creating such a garden may involve hard work initially, you will ultimately be able to enjoy a private green oasis in what was once a barren area. Such a garden is usually compact and charming, especially if it is removed from street noise. Here you can grow a range of plants in containers.

Gardening among the clouds presents different problems from those encountered at ground level. It is essential that the roof or terrace structure be solid enough to take the combined weight of soil, containers, and plants. Provision must also be made for proper drainage — plants grown in confined spaces and exposed to the full force of sun and wind need frequent watering.

The garden shown here is an aerial backyard, perched halfway up a block of apartments and offering breathtaking views over the city. It works as a genuine "outdoor room."

The structure

The terrace shown on these pages is approximately 12 x 16 ft (3.6 x 4.8 m) — the size of an average room. The starting point for the design is a crisp, no-nonsense floor of lightweight tiles, which in addition to providing unobtrusive flooring and background, allows water to drain away quickly to gutters behind the surrounding parapet walls.

Contrasting materials — thin natural stone slabs — have been used in one corner, adjoining the apartment. This change in texture raises the floor level slightly and defines an area for a small group of pots.

▶ **High-rise gardening** Open to sky, sun, and wind, this rooftop garden is an oasis of green foliage and colorful summer bedding, with views of the city landscape.

The parapet walls to either side have been topped with a simple but practical frosted-glass screen. This provides shelter from the wind — important in a terrace garden — and privacy from the adjoining apartment's garden.

The screen is a sturdy frame of 4 x 4's that supports panes of ample size; they echo the style of the adjoining window, reinforcing the link between inside and out. Frosted glass has proved a good choice, creating soft reflections that enhance the planting in the border below.

The wide parapet wall accommodates planting boxes specially constructed to fit neatly between the uprights of the screen. These boxes are deep enough for ample planting, and they provide some extra privacy at a slightly higher level than might otherwise have been possible.

◄ **Container planting** Backed by tough glass windscreens, bedding plants spill over the edges of specially constructed boxes. Silvery helichrysums and blue lobelias tumble beneath white osteospermums and red fuchsias.

▼ **Spring color** Evergreen shrubs shelter a mass of spring bulbs — hyacinths, daffodils, narcissi, tulips — and the exotic pink rosettes of camellias.

The waist-high parapet walls enclosing the roof were designed for safety but give the garden the feeling of an outdoor room. Made from wooden 4 x 4's and frosted-glass panes, they provide privacy and shelter from the wind, with only a slight loss of light.

All planting is done in containers filled with prepackaged lightweight potting mix. At this elevation, sun and wind have a particularly drying effect, and watering may be necessary several times a day during summer.

→ N

Planting at the outer parapet wall is kept deliberately low and compact to give uninterrupted views of the city. Evergreens ensure that the view, even in winter, is framed in color.

Lightweight floor tiles, laid close together and waterproofed, provide a neutral background for the planting. This floor slopes slightly, allowing surface water to drain into gutters behind the parapet walls.

The center of the garden, which enjoys a southern exposure, has been left almost completely clear. A few containers have been placed on the wall in order to break up the long horizontal line. These must be fastened securely to the masonry, however, or they might be pushed over by a gust of wind and crash on the ground below, endangering anyone passing by.

Container planting

All planting has been done in containers — wooden boxes, fiberglass tubs, and terra-cotta and plastic pots. Heavy containers have been avoided for weight reasons. At the same time there is a danger of small, light pots being knocked over by the wind; small pots also dry out quickly in this situation.

▶ **Tropical touches** Pots of fountain dracaena *(Cordyline australis)* make strong accent points among spring-flowering bulbs. These striking slow-growing evergreen shrubs rarely exceed 3 ft (90 cm) in height.

▼ **Background greenery** Algerian ivy and ornamental vines clothe the walls. Honeysuckle and summer jasmine fill the air with their sweet scents. A fan palm displays its leaves in their shade.

▲ **Specimen shrubs** Staghorn sumac makes an arresting and unusual focal point. Summer's red flower clusters turn to russet seed heads by fall and persist long after the orange-red leaves have fallen.

◀ **Conifer columns** Close to the building wall, a Chinese juniper forms a conical shape of dense gray-green foliage, soothing against the brightness of summer annuals.

The prime task of any planting plan is to provide color and interest throughout the year. This garden is wrapped around with a backdrop of permanent shrub planting, combining evergreen and deciduous species.

A staghorn sumac *(Rhus typhina)* is by far the largest of the deciduous shrubs and makes a splendid specimen with its architectural shape and foliage. This is a good container plant, as it has a tendency to throw out suckers when planted in open soil.

Evergreen plants are well represented. Two varieties of palm are on display — the fan-shaped leaves of the Chinese fan palm *(Trachycarpus fortunei)* being particularly effective.

The fountain dracaena *(Cordyline australis)* also makes a striking impact. It is an ideal plant for a pot, growing slowly and tolerating wind exposure. Because it isn't hardy north of zone 10, it must be moved indoors every fall in most of the United States. Yuccas are just as tolerant of wind and, depending on the species, may be hardy to zones 2 or 3.

Camellias, too, are superb container plants, and their glossy evergreen leaves are a welcome sight, especially in winter. They do best in light shade; avoid siting the containers in a spot facing east, where the early-spring flowers may be damaged by morning sun coming after a night of frost.

Conifers provide additional evergreen interest; dwarf and miniature junipers and chamaecyparises are ideal for container growing. Winter-flowering heathers are especially welcome during the dreariest months.

The Mexican orange *(Choisya ternata)* is a useful evergreen, with pretty white scented flowers appearing in late spring and early summer. Honeysuckle and jasmine scramble up the brickwork, softening the building's flat lines. Many honeysuckles are semievergreen, especially on a warm roof or terrace. An attractive grapevine *(Vitis vinifera)* also climbs up the wall.

Bulbs, including crocuses, narcissi, and hyacinths, are the first to flower, followed later by pots of regal lilies and summer bedding plants — a vibrant display of pelargoniums, impatiens, trailing lobelias, marigolds, and fresh white osteospermums. Annuals are used to provide instant color from spring to fall.

Several of the shrubs here are

Mediterranean in origin; gray-leaved types, such as senecio, phlomis, and helichrysum. Sun lovers, such as potentilla, *Cistus*, hebe, and hibiscus, thrive. Many herbs would also like the same exposure and enjoy dry soil. In shade, ivies and the tough evergreen elaeagnus are unrivaled.

Planning your garden

The first step to take when planning a roof or terrace garden is to explore the bearing capacity of the building. Weight will be a major consideration — anyone contemplating a roof garden should be aware that pots, containers, plants, and potting soil (even lightweight mixes) place severe pressure on the structure below.

Always consult an engineer, for while many newer buildings may be quite suitable, older structures, especially roofs, may present problems. An engineer's report will also help you secure your landlord's permission.

Adequate shelter is important — what may be a gentle breeze at street level can become a strong wind several floors up. In cities the alignment of roofs and buildings may even give rise to unexpected drafts, which can make life unpleasant for plants and people alike. In any case, careful planning and the provision of shelter are absolutely vital if young plants are not to be scorched by sun and knocked down by wind.

Shade is important if you want to sit outside for any length of time, and it may well be worthwhile to construct an arbor of wood or metal. An arbor is ideal for fragrant climbing plants and can help to screen your garden from neighbors' windows. It also makes a perfect support for hanging baskets, provided there is adequate shelter from wind.

In strong sunlight, lumber quickly dries out and preservative has to be applied more often. Roof and terrace gardens usually have little storage space, so furniture will probably have to stand outside year-round. As a result, this furniture must be durable.

Avoid painting the furniture bright white, since white will reflect sunlight in a way that is painful to the eyes. Cream is an ideal color; darker hues will absorb more sunlight and tend to become uncomfortably hot on a sunny roof or terrace.

Lawn substitutes

Turf is not a practical alternative for a roof or terrace garden, but indoor/outdoor carpeting can furnish a sort of substitute. Wooden decking is a more attractive alternative and offers relief from the hard masonry of a rooftop or terrace garden's architectural environment. (Since carpeting cannot be padded underneath, it is not especially comfortable.) Both carpeting and wooden decking can be cut into curves and free-flowing patterns that provide a feeling of space and movement.

Optional extras

You may also wish to incorporate built-in seating, raised beds, or a small sunken pool. None of these is out of the question, as long as the engineer gives the go-ahead on the roof's or terrace's load-bearing capacity.

Water can be an effective use of space, but it is nearly as heavy as soil, so a conventional pool would have to be quite small. A small fountain with a modest basin and a pump to recirculate the water might be more effective and could provide an excellent visual focal point. The sound of the water will also help block out urban noise.

In any event, having a plumber install a water faucet is essential, as regular irrigation and overhead spraying may be needed in both morning and evening during hot, dry spells.

Exterior lighting is extremely useful to extend the amount of time you can use the garden. It is best to keep it simple: a few well-positioned, unobtrusive fixtures will generally look far more attractive than imitation coach lamps, lanterns, and the like.

▶ **Outdoor rooms** Shelter is all-important for roof gardens — as protection from wind, sun, and curious neighbors. Camouflaged by climbing plants, these walls are attractive in their own right.

KNOT GARDENS

Knot gardens, popular in early colonial America, are well adapted to low-maintenance modern gardens. Their formal beauty adds a note of elegance to any landscape.

More than 200 years ago, a knot garden — a geometric pattern of closely clipped hedges — was a feature of any garden with social pretensions. Fine examples can be seen at historic restorations such as Colonial Williamsburg. Knot gardens were popular in the 1700's because they were easily maintained — periodic clipping was all the care required — and because they gratified not only the eye but also the nose: typically, the hedges were made of fragrant herbs or some aromatic shrub such as boxwood.

These same virtues make knot gardens ideal for modern garden design. Knots work especially well in small gardens, where they supply a year-round note of elegance. But they can function just as well as the focal point of a larger landscape, especially if they are planted where they can be viewed from a second-story window or an upper terrace.

Site and layout
This long, thin garden adjoins the back of an old town house and is bounded on the other three sides by walls. Next to the house is a paved sitting area, with garden furniture and potted plants.

An oval-shaped knot garden, laid out on a central axis and divided crosswise in half, extends over most of the remaining area. The two halves form a mirror image and are in themselves symmetrical. A classical stone urn set on a stone pedestal marks the center of the knot garden.

Within the simple outlines are elegant curves, arabesques, and cruciforms of boxwood, tightly grouped to form larger ornamental patterns. Bare earth in the remaining space emphasizes the sculptural quality of the boxwood

▶ **A compact knot garden** Immaculately clipped boxwood in a geometric design gives unique character to this long, narrow garden. Laburnums arching overhead raise the view above the flat embroidery of the garden floor.

and allows the geometry to be seen clearly and without interruption.

Narrow brick paths edge both long sides of the knot garden and separate it from narrow borders along the boundary walls. The long beds contain informal mixed shrub and ground-cover planting while retaining the garden's formal, architectural overtones.

Beyond the knot garden is an island bed set in an area of gravel; like the long borders, it is informally planted.

Borrowed landscape consists of overhanging laburnums from adjacent yards. Together, the trees create a small-scale imitation of the ornamental tree tunnels that were popular at the time of the first knot gardens.

The formality of a knot garden demands consistent, if infrequent, pruning of the boxwood, which has to be cut back fairly hard each year in early spring.

Weed control is also important to maintain a uniform background for the knot design — an invasion of weeds would spoil the clarity of the lines. This gardener has chosen to keep the soil surface bare inside and around the knot, accomplishing this with the help of a scuffle hoe. An even easier alternative would be blanketing the soil around the hedges with an attractive mulch, such as shredded bark.

Paths and paving

The paving has been kept intentionally simple and unobtrusive. Used, worn bricks were laid close together and end to end on a bed of sand in the simple pattern known as a stretcher bond. Running the rows of bricks crosswise, like dividing the knot garden in half crosswise, helps to stop the eye's natural tendency to race straight back to the end of this narrow space. The paths merge into gravel at the far end.

The central stone urn is also surrounded by gravel, its pale color contrasting with the green of the boxwood.

◄ **Summer highlights** The intricate scrolls and flowing arabesques of a knot garden are fully appreciated when viewed from above, each line and curve picked out in bright green. Scale can be adapted to suit gardens of all sizes; a miniature version makes a handsome centerpiece.

Boxwood edging

The dwarf boxwood (*Buxus sempervirens* 'Suffruticosa') is a traditional choice for knot gardens. A woody evergreen, it has a year-round presence, which is especially valuable in winter.

Boxwood grows slowly, so the task of clipping is manageable, and it responds well to pruning. It can be kept short or left to reach a height of about 4 ft (1.2 m). Boxwood is long-lived, lasting for many years; equally happy in sun or shade, it thrives in any kind of soil from zone 5 to 8.

Though evergreen, boxwood leaves display subtle seasonal changes. In spring the young growth is a fresh pale green, in contrast to the dark green mature foliage, giving the plant a charming two-toned effect. And though not everyone enjoys the scent, boxwood is aromatic.

General planting

Keeping with the formal theme, the knot garden is punctuated with four standard roses, planted symmetrically in the corners closest to the central urn. The urn is planted with small-leaved trailing ivies for winter interest, with flowering bulbs for spring, and with ivy-leaved geraniums for color during the rest of the year.

Ground-cover plants, including lamiums, hostas, bergenias, ornamental grasses, irises, and ferns, informally fill the narrow borders by the boundaries and the island bed. Modest ribbons of color come from pink impatiens edging the path.

Wisteria and clematis twine up the staircase and along the balcony; climbing roses are trained along the boundary walls.

Features and focal points

The knot garden centers on a classical stone urn. Immediately beyond the knot garden is another stone urn on a fluted pedestal. At the other end, a potted standard rose pleasantly reinforces the garden's symmetry.

▶ **Winter spectacular** A knot garden in evergreen boxwood is attractive throughout the year, but it looks truly magnificent with a dusting of frost or snow, when the design reveals itself in simple formality. Boxwood is naturally compact and responds well to regular clipping and topiary designs.

**KNOT GARDEN
DESIGNS**

▲ ▼ **Square designs** Simple lines work well in knot garden patterns. A square grid of plain green boxwood, filled in with gravel, is punctuated with perfectly clipped spheres of golden boxwood.

▼ **Diamond patterns** Ground-cover plants — prostrate roses and nepetas — fill the spaces. Bedding plants, such as impatiens, wax begonias, ageratums, and French marigolds, may also be used.

To add touches of color and soften the formality, groups of terra-cotta flower pots hold seasonal bedding plants.

Getting started

A knot garden's pattern should be immediately obvious, or the overall effect will be lost. Experiment on graph paper, drawing the knot to scale. Allow 8 in (20 cm) for the width of boxwood or herbal hedges. If you intend to leave bare earth in the spaces between hedges or add a mulch layer there, the hedges may come close to each other. You may, however, wish to fill these spaces with ornamental plantings — annual flowers, bulbs, or even different-colored lettuces (an unusual and striking spring cover). In that case, leave at least 1½ ft (45 cm) between the hedges.

Try one geometric shape within another: a circle within a square, perhaps with a central cross. Alternatively, try circles within circles or squares within squares; use diagonals to create diamonds or triangles. Working out a design that suits you *and* the site may take some time. Simple designs are often the best.

When you are satisfied with the design, peg out the pattern on the soil. A peg with a piece of string attached can be used to give the circumference of a circle. For a small knot garden, you could cover the area with woven or spun plastic landscape cloth, which is designed to suppress weeds but to admit air and water to the soil. Then draw the design and plant through the plastic before covering the surfaces in between with gravel or mulch.

Boxwoods should be spaced 9 in (23 cm) apart. Buying plants from a garden center is likely to be expensive, but you will have a garden feature of great character that could last for generations.

You can save money by raising plants from boxwood cuttings, perhaps obtained from a friend's prunings. Rooted in a cold frame in late summer, the cuttings should be grown on in a nursery bed for a couple of years before being planted out permanently.

You could also use lavender or santolina in a knot garden design.

They are less formal than boxwood but especially suitable for interfilling with other herbs.

Knot garden fillings
In old English knot gardens, spaces in the design were filled with honesty, sweet William, pansy, narcissus, violet, rose, lily, marigold, columbine, and primrose. Sometimes they were planted with a mossy carpet of turf or low-growing herbs.

▶ **A knot of herbs** 'Hidcote' lavender is used to trace this Elizabethan design. Pots of sweet cicely on a gravel base are grouped around a focal point of aromatic bay laurel clipped into a pyramid shape.

Potager, the art of planting vegetables and herbs in decorative geometric patterns within low boxwood hedges, was popular in the 16th century. Much later the Victorians filled knot gardens with colorful summer annuals and tender bedding plants.

Filling knot gardens with plants provides color, fragrance,

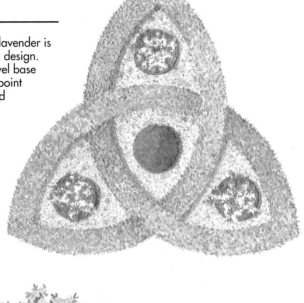

▼ **Circular theme** Triangular segments make up a traditional pattern. The centerpiece in this knot garden is a weeping standard rose, with the green-and-yellow theme repeated in the filling of lady's-mantle *(Alchemilla mollis)*.

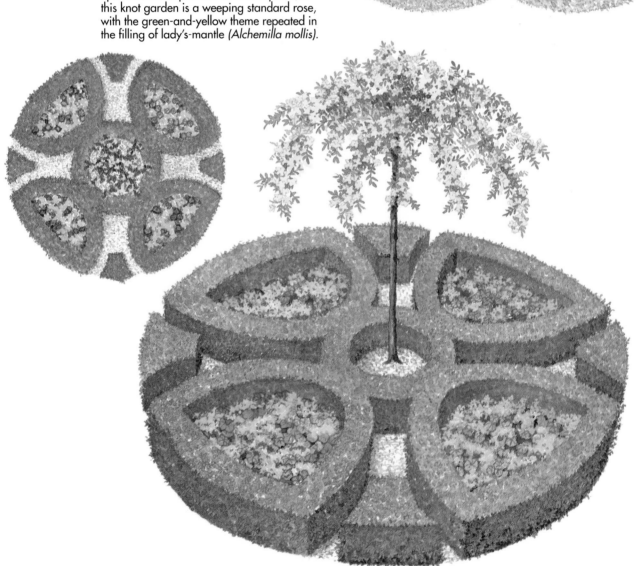

◄ **Centerpiece** The visual impact of a knot garden is heightened with a central vertical feature that rises above, yet unites, the individual segments. The focal point can be a sundial, a clipped topiary specimen in boxwood or yew, a statue, or a tripod of roses.

Formal parterres in the great estates of yesteryear often made a feature of intricate knot gardens arranged around a large water fountain. In the average modern garden, a birdbath or a simple urn filled with bright bedding plants seems more fitting.

and seasonal interest, but the clarity of the design can be lost unless low-growing plants are used. Choose plants that can fend for themselves rather than those needing constant attention — working conditions are likely to be uncomfortably cramped.

Colored sand, stones, earth, ashes, brick dust, or chalk often replaced flowers in early knot gardens to create flat, abstract patterns of color. Purists even replaced the edging plants with wooden strips.

A modern version could be made, in a simple square or diamond pattern, using gravels, colored paving stones, interlocking concrete pavers, or bricks.

Alternative edgings

Before boxwood became popular, dwarf aromatic herbs were used: lavender, thrift, rosemary, hyssop, marjoram, santolina, thyme, or mint. Many were short-lived and needed frequent clipping to remain compact. The clippings were often strewed on floors to mask the smell of that era's poor sanitation.

If you don't mind the extra

lifting, dividing, replanting, and pruning involved, a herb-edged knot garden is pretty. Various kinds of colorful vegetables, such as ruby and green chards, can be made to serve this purpose, too.

Introducing focal points

A vertical feature automatically enlivens a knot garden's low, flat plane of greenery. In a small knot garden, one central plant or ornament is enough; larger gardens can have several focal points, perhaps with slightly smaller features set in the corners.

Stone fountains are traditional, but sundials, birdbaths, statues, small stone seats, planters, or urns all work well.

Plants that are naturally columnar or are trained or grafted into upright shapes make good focal points: for example, junipers and Irish yews; standard bay laurels, fuchsias, and pelargoniums; and grafted standard roses and weeping cotoneasters.

Boxwood and yew topiaries make excellent focal points in a knot garden; as variations on the theme of formally clipped evergreen plants, they can create a

pleasantly unified and old-fashioned feeling.

Historical footnote

Apart from the attraction of having a feature with such unique character in your garden, a knot garden gives a real sense of garden history. Since Roman times, formal gardens of clipped plants have been featured in many of the famous gardens of the world.

Medieval monastic herb gardens were subdivided into orderly rectangular beds, but more for practicality than beauty. The Renaissance, with its interest in classical culture, revived the art of clipped ornamental gardens.

Knot gardens spread from Italy to France, Holland, and England, and from there to America. In Europe they were replaced by a more natural style of garden in the 18th century, but they remained popular in America for a couple of generations longer, especially in the South.

The Victorians loved knot gardening, and many Victorian parks still display them. Recently there has been a revival of interest in knot garden designs.

ORIENTAL WATER GARDENS

Eastern garden designs contrast open spaces with crowded areas and stillness with movement in order to create a mood of tranquillity.

The finest gardens are more often than not a happy coincidence of a good site, a sympathetic eye, and a genuine feel for plants. Occasionally, though, a designer aims for a specific goal and achieves something quite special.

In this case an average suburban garden, neglected for many years, was transformed into a peaceful retreat with an Oriental feeling. The design proves that even a temperate-climate garden can have a truly Eastern flavor.

Water is a special feature of the garden, as it nearly always is in the East. The centerpiece is a wedge-shaped pool that reflects the contrasting shapes of surrounding foliage marvelously. Wood decking, set at different levels and angles around the pool and sitting area, is reminiscent of the raised wooden houses typical of Southeast Asia. A movable collection of potted plants, subtle plant forms, and delicate bamboo handrails augment the mood.

The materials used for the furnishings have a natural, honest simplicity; they are handled with a quiet confidence and precise attention to detail — the stepping-stones set in gravel, for instance, fit the overall mood and are thoroughly practical.

The assignment
The initial task in garden design is a basic site appraisal. Here the lot is long and narrow — 82 ft x 33 ft (25 m x 10 m) — bounded by a road on one side and another garden on the other. Outbuildings stand at the bottom of the lot, while the rear of the house faces north, casting shadow over the area nearest the house wall. The

▼ **Eastern atmosphere** A small suburban garden, enclosed by rush-covered screens, captures the essence of Oriental design philosophy, with water, wood, and plant forms at its center.

site is essentially flat, the boundaries rectangular.

The commission called for a low-maintenance garden with color and year-round interest. The garden was to have an essentially Oriental feeling, with a strong emphasis on water.

Ample room for sitting, dining, and entertaining was a basic requirement, and access to the outbuildings was needed. A hot tub close to the house was also wanted — a feature common in many Eastern cultures. The hot tub is connected to the domestic water and heating supplies and incorporates a pump and water filter.

With any long, narrow garden, one of the main tasks is to create a feeling of space and movement, leading the eye away from the boundaries and breaking the space down into more manageable sections. As the rear of the house remains in shade for much of the day, it made sense to position the main sitting area where it would be able to catch the sun at the far end of the garden, adjoining the outbuildings. The sitting area is linked to the house by a series of walkways.

The space is nearly three times as long as it is wide, so it was organized into a corresponding number of "rooms," with each section roughly equal in size, to detract from the overall length.

Wooden decking

The most important outdoor room is the wooden deck in the back; it serves as a sitting area and surrounds the pool. This sort of garden floor is not only easy and relatively inexpensive to install, it is also part of the Oriental tradition. Here it has been used with great flair to form a stylish framework set at different angles and levels to make the most of a fairly restricted space.

For a wooden deck to wear well and continue to look good in a damp, temperate climate, careful construction is essential. There must be adequate ventilation beneath the deck, and sturdy floor joists should be bolted to posts set into concrete.

▶ **Wood and water** Natural elements are all-important in traditional Japanese gardens, as is a hint of mystery. Although it seems simple, this garden is the result of the endless attention to detail that creates harmony.

The type of lumber used for the framing and decking can vary: softwood is fine if it has been pressure-treated with a preservative. A naturally rot-resistant wood, such as Western red cedar, is more attractive and will last well but costs more.

The boards are set at an angle to lead feet and eyes on a diagonal axis across the garden. Diagonal lines are the longest length across a rectangle and therefore give a feeling of increased space. The angled walkways create interesting diversions and are far more effective than a path leading straight up and down the garden would be.

While the deck floor has been stained a dark brown, the boundaries are covered with light-colored woven rush screen panels — an admirable way to hide unsightly surfaces in such a setting and the perfect foil for planting. Rush matting also covers the outside of the shed, merging it into the overall composition and increasing the illusion of a Far Eastern environment.

The decked area beneath the wooden pergola is set square with the boundaries, forming a more conventional, static space across the width of the garden, with the deck dropping down in a single broad step to the pool.

Water features

A pool is obligatory in such a setting. This calm stretch of water not only captures reflections from the sky and poolside plants but also subdivides the terrace from the softer parts of the garden that lead back toward the house.

The black butyl rubber liner used for the pool gives an impression of depth and mystery. A liner works well here, being easily tucked up under the decking on three sides and into a beach of loose pebbles on the other.

To add to the Oriental theme, koi carp swim in the pool. The colors of these fish vary enormously, from gold to black and white. They grow large in time — and are tame enough to be fed by hand.

Excavated soil from the pool was used to create a rock garden, and the liner was extended to make a stream bed that flows back into the pool, using power from a submersible pump. Gently lapping water provides soothing sounds in the garden.

A wooden bridge spans the water, the plain bamboo handrail echoing the natural material used in the boundary screen. A main strength of this garden is the way plantings and furnishings complement each other. For example, the bridge is aligned to focus on a

N ↑

The irregularly shaped pool is lined with tough black butyl rubber and stocked with rushes, water lilies, and koi carp. Open to the sky, the decked edge is wide enough for sunbathing and relaxation.

Wooden decking is set at different angles and levels to make interesting walkways through the garden. Occasional scrubbing is required to keep it free of dangerous slippery algae.

The planting emphasizes foliage rather than flowers, with a pleasing variety of plant shapes and contrasting leaf forms. Plants in pots add extra flexibility to a small garden, since they can be moved about to create different effects.

HOUSE

Stepping-stones set in gravel meander pleasantly through lush planting. Though they look random, they have been placed quite precisely to make the most of a small space. From an open area, the path narrows to a single line through lush foliage that partly obscures the rest of the garden.

◄ **Wooden deck** The raised wooden deck extends to the pool's edge, where a bridge offers a perch from which to contemplate the still water. A black pool liner gives an illusion of depth and reflects the open sky above.

► **Moisture lovers** Wetland plants by the pool edge include golden-flowered marsh marigold *(Caltha palustris palustris)* and the plantainlike *Alisma plantago-aquatica,* with dainty white flower sprays. The massive leaf clumps contrast charmingly with the feathery foliage of mountain ash by the rush-covered fence.

▼ **Mirror images** A still sheet of water is disturbed only by colorful koi carp darting among clumps of rushes and breaking the reflection of sky and overhead trees.

Planting

The owner of the garden knows much about plants, and the trees were carefully chosen.

The purple-leaved birch (*Betula pendula* 'Purpurea') is a slow-growing, rather delicate tree that needs a sheltered environment. The birch makes a handsome contrast to the golden privet and to the rich green of the marsh marigolds *(Caltha palustris palustris)* at the pool edges.

Another well-chosen tree with an elegant spreading habit is mountain ash *(Sorbus vilmorinii)*. The foliage is superb in fall, when it turns purple and red, and the fruit is attractive too, borne in loose, drooping clusters that change color with age from deep pink to almost white. In time the tree branches will droop gracefully over the bridge. A decidedly Oriental choice is the Japanese cherry (*Prunus serrulata* 'Shirofugen'), with flowers that open white and fade to a delicate pale purple among young copper-colored leaves.

The shrubs are a mixture of deciduous and evergreen species, with fatsia and privet making a bold show in winter. Of the bamboos, *Pseudosasa japonica* is particularly fine. The leaf margins of another bamboo, *Sasa palmata*, can die off in winter, giving it at first glance an attractive variegation. It's a fairly rampant bamboo and needs to be kept in check. The grass *Miscanthus sacchariflorus* is also vigorous, reaching 6½ ft (2 m) in a short time.

Planting at the lower level concentrates on hardy perennials that thrive in the moist soil by the waterside. There's a fine selection of hosta, ligularia, caltha, trollius, and rodgersia.

Two specimens of pyracantha and yucca were saved from the former garden; both offered welcome greenery as the new plants were becoming established and now make fine evergreen accent plants.

Pots are a versatile feature in the garden — and reminiscent of the East — as portable containers for instant color from spring bulbs and summer annuals and for more permanent plantings, too. Container plants include *Fatsia japonica,* with its large leaves, and the delightful *Caragana arborescens,* which bears pealike flowers in late spring.

fine yucca, one of the few plants retained from the former garden.

Paths and paving

The bridge marks a transition in the garden, leading from the essentially hard landscape of the deck, pergola, and pool to the softer, planted area negotiated by stepping-stones. The plants form a tension point, with two wings of foliage almost closing together and heightening the change of mood.

The stepping-stones are laid with great skill; the loose pebbles are a perfect foil to crisp paving slabs and plants. Apparently laid at random, the paving slabs perform a precise function, linking the exit from the house to the far-end deck in a meandering line that increases the sense of spaciousness, as well as mystery as the path suddenly narrows and ends at the entrance to the deck.

Near the house the informality of random steps gives way to carefully laid slabs in straight lines that lead across to the hot tub. As elsewhere in the garden, the attention to detail is complete: the pebbles are set in mortar and laid tightly together to give a sense of natural order in the area beside the house.

The hot tub is neatly screened from the rest of the garden. It is wrapped around in soft foliage and partly sunk into the decking, with a raised platform to give access to the tub, and sheltered by rush matting. Covered over when not in use, the tub is drained in wintertime.

In the dining area, tables and chairs have been chosen to blend with the decking and overhead beams. This is the ultimate outdoor room, used extensively for entertaining and relaxation.

In a garden that relies heavily on the texture and juxtaposition of foliage rather than flowers, a yellow umbrella over the table echoes the color of the golden privet and the majestic spires of *Ligularia.*

153

The pots themselves are chosen to complement particular plants. Though many of them are Oriental, the rest are a varied mix collected over the years.

Overall, the plants and the hardscape are in perfect harmony, with a juxtaposition of natural and manufactured features supporting one another to produce a delightful outside room.

The garden is easy to care for; the only real work is maintenance of the decking and gentle disciplining of some of the vigorous plants, which might otherwise upset the balance.

▶ **Contrasting leaf textures** Foliage plants dominate in Oriental gardens. A giant miscanthus, its grassy leaves trembling in the breeze, contrasts in color, shape, and texture with the rigid, spine-tipped leaf blades of a yucca.

▼ **Hot tub** A recent fashion in the West, hot tubs are a long-cherished feature of Japanese culture, providing a means of relaxation in natural surroundings.

MEDITERRANEAN GARDENS

White walls, terra-cotta pots, gravel, and an abundance of sun-loving plants give this formal garden a strong Mediterranean feeling.

This gravel-mulched garden is surrounded on all four sides by high walls. They have been whitewashed and are topped with terracotta tiles, which instantly create a Mediterranean atmosphere.

Plants from that part of the world tend to be both heat and drought resistant, which makes them ideal for the climates of the Southwest and the southern California coast. However, a Mediterranean garden works well in most sunny spots wherever winters are not severe.

Originally the site shown here was sloping, with a 3 ft (90 cm) drop across the width of the garden. The soil is clayey and strongly alkaline, and it becomes rockhard in summer. In winter it is cold and wet, though not waterlogged. The south-facing site is sunny, and the pale walls reflect heat as well as provide shelter

from harsh winds, making this a perfect spot for tender plants.

The layout

The design, roughly a cross shape, is based on rectangles and squares. An ornamental cherry tree (*Prunus* species), growing in a central position at the junction of four wide gravel paths, is the pivot of the layout, creating a pleasing asymmetry.

Raised beds provide not only the perfect drainage that sun-loving alpine and gray-leaved plants need but also the opportunity to create a formal, geometric pattern in three dimensions. The use of railroad ties, an easy-to-assemble and relatively inexpensive material for retaining walls, reinforces the linear quality of the design. Although not part of the original plan, one of the raised beds running along the length of

a boundary wall is used as a nursery and for propagation.

A pergola along one wall creates a shady walkway, provides support for climbing roses, and helps conceal less-than-perfect views outside the garden. Running parallel to the north-facing perimeter wall, the pergola is a freestanding structure, designed to let light and air circulate freely among the climbing plants, thus reducing the incidence of disease.

Access and an attractive view into the garden from a courtyard are gained through an archway in a newly built whitewashed wall.

▼ **Mediterranean flavor** Whitewashed walls surround this sun-filled garden, which is lavishly stocked with foliage and flowering plants tumbling over the edges of raised beds. A mature cherry tree casts dappled shade.

A second archway, framed by vigorous wall shrubs, leads into another section, a well-tended kitchen garden.

A collection of troughs and old sinks, some of stone and others of porcelain coated with a mixture of adhesive, peat, and cement to imitate weathered stone, makes a distinctive feature in one corner. They display sun-loving alpines, mostly summer-flowering hens and chickens (*Sempervivum* species), many of which are grown individually in shallow terra-cotta containers.

Small groupings of stone boulders imitate a miniature mountainside. Of sculptural interest, they contrast in scale with the gravel and in form with the raised rectangular planting beds. Along the south-facing paved sitting area is a larger alpine meadow, complete with rocks and gravel mulch and home to clumps of colorful alpines and dwarf shrubs.

At the end of the rock garden, a low wooden seat gives views of the entire garden and catches the late-afternoon sun.

Construction materials

The sloping site was leveled by cutting and filling, with a small amount of excavated soil moved to another plot. Three walls already existed. To complete the enclosure, a fourth wall was built of concrete blocks, which were stuccoed and tiled to blend in with the other walls.

One large tree, a sugar maple (*Acer saccharum*), was removed from the back of the site to maximize the available sunlight, but the flowering cherry was retained as the garden's focal point.

The raised beds were created with used railroad ties but could easily have been made from pressure-treated landscape timbers. The retaining walls are two or three ties high and laid on a foundation of "dead men," or short ties set crosswise in the ground. The lowest level of full ties is set slightly below ground level to hide the foundation and increase the wall's stability.

The pergola is made of pressure-treated poles. Any cut sections have been re-treated. The poles, which were sunk straight into the ground, show no signs of rot. (Concrete foundations for wooden poles sometimes cause, rather than prevent, rot, as water

A mature cherry tree acts as the central focal point. Clean, angular lines provided by long lengths of railroad tie add a formal touch to the design. Raised beds aid drainage — vital for sun-loving Mediterranean plants. Extensive areas of gravel contribute to the atmosphere.

Topped by red tiles, an archway breaks the expanse of whitewashed wall. Pink-and-white climbing roses frame the opening, and tall foxgloves (*Digitalis purpurea*) add height to the planting. A tree peony thrives in the sheltered spot.

N

Stone troughs and terra-cotta bowls enhance the garden's Mediterranean aura. Planted with a variety of hens and chickens, they provide evergreen interest and, in summer, pink flowers. Grouped together, large limestone boulders create a natural ornamental feature.

A rustic pergola, covered with climbing roses, runs along one boundary. Providing pleasant shade, it ends with a simple focal point — a large terra-cotta jar. The path consists of railroad ties, their edges hidden by thickly planted London pride *(Saxifraga umbrosa).*

A nursery bed occupies one raised border along a sunny, sheltered boundary wall. Shrubs, including a tree aster *(Olearia),* break up the nursery rows of young plants. The wall is covered with *Clematis montana* and *C. orientalis.*

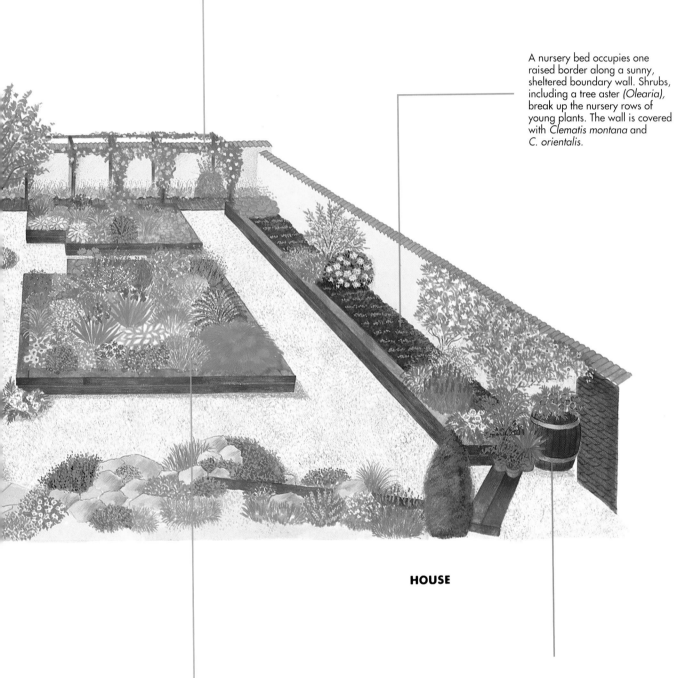

HOUSE

Raised beds are filled with a variety of perennials, alpines, bulbs, and low shrubs. Around the edges, ground cover is provided by many summer-flowering plants, such as bellflowers *(Campanula carpatica).* Vertical accents come from ornamental grasses.

A large wooden barrel holds a tomato plant as a backdrop to a collection of terra-cotta pots planted with colorful fuchsias and variegated New Zealand flax *(Phormium tenax).* The composition is balanced by a conical Lawson cypress *(Chamaecyparis lawsoniana* 'Ellwoodii').

can become trapped in the tiny space between the pole and the concrete.) Under the pergola runs a railroad tie path, half a tie wide, bedded on sand.

Gravel is a less costly alternative to more expensive forms of paving. The area to be surfaced in this way was first treated with a weed killer, then given a foundation of crushed rock and stone fines, and finally covered with a 1 in (2.5 cm) thick layer of pea gravel, which is raked level often. The large ornamental stone boulders are limestone.

Planting schemes

This is essentially a plant collector's garden, and plants take precedence here over furnishings. The choice of plants is dictated by the sheltered, sunny site and the fast-draining, alkaline soil.

It is very much a summer garden, early summer in particular, when most of the alpine plants come into bloom. At other times of the year, color comes from winter- and spring-flowering bulbs, such as winter-flowering irises, crocuses, and species tulips, as well as the lush growth of several ornamental grasses. If you face

the garden from the courtyard arch, you see colors that range from stronger, richer ones on the left of the path to paler, softer ones on the right.

The garden includes old-fashioned and modern shrub roses and mixed climbers along the walls. Some are fragrant, and all are soft in color. These climbers help to break up the large area of wall and include white-flowered

▲ **Evergreen hens and chickens** A collection of shallow pots holds a large range of sempervivums, displaying a variety of forms and colors against a weathered stone trough "planted" with large limestone rocks.

▼ **Planting beds** Raised beds constructed from railroad ties ensure the perfect soil drainage essential for alpines. Flower colors are soft and muted among strong foliage that runs from dark green to silvery gray.

▶ **Terra-cotta theme** A tile-topped archway gives glimpses into the walled kitchen garden. Climbing roses clothe the walls, and at ground level pots of alpine plants and pea gravel repeat the color scheme of the wall.

common jasmine *(Jasminum officinale), Clematis montana,* and *C. orientalis.*

Along the southern boundary wall, London pride *(Saxifraga umbrosa)* dominates the planting under the pergola. The plants, taking advantage of the lightly shaded site, produce dainty clusters of pink flowers into late spring. The pergola itself supports climbing roses; at one end, an upturned terra-cotta jar adds an authentic Mediterranean flavor, its color bringing warmth to the dark evergreen foliage of *Stranvaesia davidiana.* This foliage turns crimson in fall, complementing the drooping clusters of red berries that follow the white early-summer flowers.

The raised beds are densely planted with sun-loving plants that thrive in the free-draining soil. Low-growing plants are concentrated around the edges of the beds and include tussock bellflowers *(Campanula carpatica),* Jacob's ladder *(Polemonium carneum),* and prickly poppy *(Argemone mexicana),* which produces orange or red flowers.

Central accents are formed by taller plants, such as New Zealand flax *(Phormium tenax)* and several black pines *(Pinus nigra)* that reinforce the garden's Mediterranean flavor. Foxgloves *(Digitalis purpurea)* echo the vertical lines of the eastern archway.

Maintenance

This unusual type of garden requires a maintenance regime similar to that of other gardens, with one or two exceptions. The beds need weeding, but weeds in the thick layer of gravel are rarely troublesome. Cultivated plants and some wild plants, such as foxglove, that self-sow in the gravel become part of the garden scene.

▶ **Pergola walk** Sweetly scented roses clamber over a framework of poles, with clusters of pink-flowered London pride at their feet. At the end of the vista, a large upturned terra-cotta jar stands in front of the wall.

▲ **Mediterranean plants** Trees and shrubs native to the mountains of southern Europe revel in this sunny enclosed garden. From the archway a black pine *(Pinus nigra)* surveys clumps of sprawling bright-colored rockroses *(Cistus).*

▶ **Barrels of tomatoes** A trailing tomato spills down over pots of hardy fuchsias. On the wall above, a vigorous hybrid clematis dangles its clawlike purple-striped blossoms.

Watering is done regularly in hot, dry weather because raised beds dry out quickly. The plants growing in the troughs and shallow pots and in the rock garden are largely drought resistant.

The sheltered environment protects several frost-sensitive plants. They are given no special protection, but cuttings are taken from those that may not survive the winter, such as black horehound *(Ballota pseudodictamnus)* and twinspur *(Diascia barberae).* The cuttings are kept in a cool greenhouse over winter and planted out the following spring.

This Mediterranean-style garden was neither difficult nor time-consuming to create, and a similar design would suit any sunny site.

TOPIARY FRAMEWORK

Adding a note of whimsy or formality to large or small gardens, topiary serves as living, self-repairing sculpture.

Though commonly perceived as appropriate to large estates, topiary serves just as well in modest backyards. A carefully clipped yew or bay tree is well within the resources of any gardener.

Topiary is easy to include in any garden, and it can be adapted to almost any design, used either as a major feature or as an isolated focal point.

Being woody and usually evergreen, topiary is a valuable partner for more transient flowers — annuals, biennials, bulbs, perennials, and herbs. In season these plants display their foliage and flowers against the formal lines of topiary. In winter the topiary may provide the only interest, focusing the eye when herbaceous plants are dormant.

Formal clipped hedges can pro-vide living fencing, backdrops, screens, internal walls, or edging, according to location and height. An existing hedge can be made more decorative if pruned to form crenellations or finials along the top. Freestanding topiary sculptures can provide focal points, or they can set up pleasing rhythms when arranged in pairs or rows.

A topiary corridor

The garden shown here combines topiary hedging and freestanding sculptures. It is a section of a larger garden, but the layout could easily be self-contained. With a little adjustment, the design could suit gardens of different proportions, and any part of it could provide inspiration for a small area.

Long, narrow lots can make awkward gardens, but this thin strip of land has been transformed into a splendid topiary display, surrounded by a tapestry of herbs. The simple symmetrical plan reflects the formality of the topiary and is based on interlocking rectangles and circles.

The layout consists of a narrow central brick-edged gravel path and an old millstone surrounded

---

▼ **Green corridor** A long, narrow lot has been transformed into a sunny corridor of closely clipped yew hedges formalized with curves and rounded finials. Free-standing boxwood spirals stand sentry in the corners, and rounded domes of golden boxwood accentuate borders of herbs.

Brick-edged gravel paths and an open center reinforce the design.

Boxwood spirals stand like sentinels in each corner of the garden. These four freestanding sculptures, each corkscrewing out of the ground, guard the entrance and exit.

by a wide gravel circle at the halfway point. This widening out of the central area creates a feeling of generous space in spite of the narrowness of the lot.

Narrow, easily maintained beds border both the path and the central circle. At one end of the garden, flagstone paving laid at right angles to the path creates a T-shaped sitting area.

Framework planting

Tall, clipped yew hedges enclose the garden, providing shelter and privacy. At the far end the hedge is lower, clipped into curves and with a gap that affords views beyond the garden. The curves end in ball-shaped finials, marking the entry to the topiary garden.

The ball theme is repeated in three pairs of clipped ball-shaped

▲ **Foliage contrasts** Golden boxwood shaped into a well-rounded sphere punctuates the edge of the central circle. Bright green mint, its roots contained in a terra-cotta pot, repeats the circular theme, and the graceful leaf fronds and yellow flower clusters of fennel tower above.

shrubs of golden boxwood at regular intervals along the path.

Four spiral-trained boxwood trees are planted symmetrically, one in each corner of the garden, to contrast with the golden ball shapes and with the sprawling herbs surrounding them.

The topiary sculptures are all carefully tended and in excellent condition. A disadvantage of topiary — particularly where a shape is repeated — is that any flaws quickly become obvious.

Handsome containers reinforce
the circular elements in the
garden. The terra-cotta pots
are more than decorative. They
contain herbs that would be
too invasive in open ground.

Walls of evergreen yew enclose
the narrow lot to give shelter and
seclusion. The ends are clipped
into curves and topped with ball-
shaped finials to create an
elegant vista.

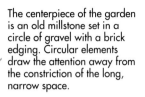

The centerpiece of the garden
is an old millstone set in a
circle of gravel with a brick
edging. Circular elements
draw the attention away from
the constriction of the long,
narrow space.

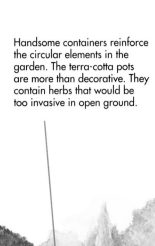

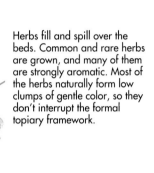

Herbs fill and spill over the
beds. Common and rare herbs
are grown, and many of them
are strongly aromatic. Most of
the herbs naturally form low
clumps of gentle color, so they
don't interrupt the formal
topiary framework.

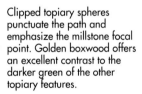

Clipped topiary spheres
punctuate the path and
emphasize the millstone focal
point. Golden boxwood offers
an excellent contrast to the
darker green of the other
topiary features.

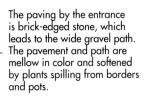

The paving by the entrance
is brick-edged stone, which
leads to the wide gravel path.
The pavement and path are
mellow in color and softened
by plants spilling from borders
and pots.

Yew, boxwood, and privet are the plants best suited to achieve the density and precision needed for topiary work, as they are small leaved, evergreen, and responsive to pruning. Hornbeam or beech could be substituted for the yew hedge; they grow faster but provide no winter greenery, though both retain attractive rich brown leaves through winter.

Tall bay trees trained into a flame shape or naturally erect Irish yews or Irish junipers would give roughly the same effect as the spiral topiary forms, but without their precision. Also, dwarf arborvitaes and chamaecyparises with naturally round growth habits could be used instead of the clipped ball-shaped boxwoods in this garden.

Herbal tapestry

With the exception of mazes, few gardens are based entirely on topiary. A blend of topiary and nontopiary plants, in fact, enhances both types of plant. In this sunny site with well-drained soil, medicinal, culinary, and cosmetic herbs fill and spill over the borders in a range of green, gold, silver, purple, and gray foliage in plain and variegated forms.

For a garden on a smaller scale, the choice could be limited to the more useful culinary herbs, perhaps with an exception made for lavender. More invasive herbs, such as mint and lemon balm, are best contained in pots.

Popular kitchen and ornamental herbs grown here include fennel, chives, thyme, rosemary, sage, garlic, tarragon, mint, marjoram, and lavender. More unusual herbs are grown, too, such as sorrel, wormwood, anise, angelica, hyssop, coriander, borage, woodruff, and burnet. In addition, herb-filled terra-cotta pots are strategically placed in the central circle to reinforce the symmetry.

Even at the peak of their flowering, herbs produce modest blossoms and gentle color: the yellows of silver-leaved daisy-family herbs, such as artemisias; the mauves of lavender and mints; and the greenish whites and yellows of umbellifers, such as angelica. Most of these herbs are excellent for attracting butterflies and bees.

For a brighter show of flowers, which would work equally well within a topiary framework, a mixture of annuals, herbaceous perennials, and bulbs could be substituted.

Both herb and perennial flower gardens are labor-intensive, involving weeding, lifting and dividing, and possibly staking and replacing. To cut down the workload without losing color, the beds could be filled with low-growing shrubs and ground-cover plants.

Tall plants should be avoided, since they tend to interrupt the clean, geometric lines of the topiary and may make the task of clipping the hedges difficult.

A third, more subtle, arrangement would be to replace the ornamental plants with a grass or chamomile lawn. Dwarf boxwood could then edge the path, emphasizing the architectural quality of the design. Such edging blends with formal or informal designs.

▲ **Topiary shapes** Symmetrical spirals can be created by twisting the main stem of a supple young boxwood — or yew — around a stake, but it will take several years to achieve the desired effect. For quicker results, cheat slightly by choosing a more mature plant and clipping it to shape.

Mark out a wide spiral shape with two lengths of string, and carefully clip the foliage away right to the main stem. Maintain the shape by trimming at least once a year.

▶ **Yew walls** Close-clipped yew hedges enclose a scene of seclusion and quiet contemplation. Circular shapes — spiraling green boxwood, spheres of golden boxwood, and rounded yew finials by the entrance — reduce the potential for monotony.

An old millstone set within a gravel circle widens the perspective, and on the paved sitting area, a miniature stone pool marvelously mirrors the drifting clouds.

◀ **Boxwood spheres** Rows of green boxwood trimmed to perfect spheres follow the lines of a long rose pergola, and ribbons of dwarf boxwood edge the path beneath.

Such topiary features can easily be adapted to suit gardens of more modest size. The shapes are easy to maintain and will continue to provide interest long after the roses have passed their glorious prime.

▼ **Topiary duck** Fashioned from golden privet, a duck sculpture strikes a lighthearted note. Animal and bird shapes demand both skill and patience. To make the task easier, you can use galvanized wire forms available at some garden centers. Start, however, with simple geometric shapes — cubes, spheres, and pyramids — before attempting these complex forms.

Topiary shapes

In topiary, plants are treated like clay — raw material to be formed into a wide variety of shapes. As with clay, some topiary shapes — such as spheres, cubes, cones, and pyramids, plus simple forms of edging — are easier to execute than others. These tend to be the most popular forms of topiary and are ideal for the beginner.

Ribbons of dwarf shrubs such as boxwood, planted single file or in tightly staggered rows, can follow almost any curve or series of straight lines and angles. A dwarf boxwood edging can form right angles with great precision.

Ribbon edging can be square in cross section, tapered near the top, or rounded. An edging prevents border plants from spilling over the lawn edge or paving. It also allows light to reach them and their beauty to be seen.

Edging on either side of a path, especially where the path runs through flower borders, is traditional in formal garden designs.

Spheres, also called globes or balls, are pleasing to the eye from every direction. They can be freestanding or grown as finials topping formal hedges.

Topiary spheres can be any size, though miniature spheres look best in containers — otherwise they may disappear into the general garden melee.

Pairs or rows of spheres can repeat the rhythm set up by nearby features, such as pergolas, or create a rhythm of their own. If a shape is repeated, each plant must look healthy and as similar as possible to the others. Misshapen or undersized specimens stand out like missing teeth.

Arches in topiary are especially impressive and can be trained over a freestanding metal framework or as a continuation of a hedge. Arches are long-term projects, since a height of about 6 ft (1.8 m) must be reached before the final shaping takes place.

Animals form the whimsical side of topiary. They can range from friendly little birds to elegant peacocks or strange mythological beasts.

Animals are the hardest shapes to form — it's difficult to make them look realistic, even when they are trained over galvanized wire forms.

JAPANESE GARDENS

The essence of a Japanese garden captures nature itself, using stones, water, and colorful trees and shrubs.

A Western suburb may seem an unlikely spot for an authentic Japanese garden, but this example shows what can be achieved in such a setting. Although the owner is a horticulturist, he had no specialized knowledge of Japanese gardening when he began. His main asset was enthusiasm, and he built up the garden over many years, learning as he went along.

Japanese gardens are usually designed to be viewed from the house, with secondary views from pavilions, bridges, or special viewing stones.

The site
The lot is a self-contained rectangular back garden, approximately 60 ft x 40 ft (18 m x 12 m), in the midst of a modest suburban development. It was originally planted as lawn, with straight flower borders along the sides, and included a small rock garden, which has since been enlarged.

The south-facing garden is fairly sheltered. Additional shelter is provided by woven bamboo panels, 6 ft (1.8 m) high, attached to conventional perimeter fencing. The soil is neutral in pH and reasonably moisture retentive.

Planning and development
Unlike many gardens, which begin with a master plan, this one developed gradually from a single Japanese feature. The inspiration was a group of three shrubs: *Pieris japonica* 'Variegata,' a silver-variegated evergreen shrub; a Japanese maple (*Acer palmatum* 'Dissectum'); and a dwarf Hinoki cypress (*Chamaecyparis obtusa* 'Nana').

The owner was unaware of their shared Oriental origins but found the combination of their forms and foliage pleasing.

Soon afterwards a visit to the Japanese garden in a local botanical garden prompted the purchase of a Buddha statue, and that inspired the owner to enlarge upon the Japanese theme. Since then, more Oriental plants and features have been added.

Philosophy and design
Every feature in a Japanese garden is symbolic, whether of a concept, such as long life, or an element of nature, such as a mountain. Often a single feature will symbolize several ideas, on different levels. Rocks and water are of great importance.

Miniaturization plays a crucial part in Japanese gardens, in which many features must be contained within a small space. Formality and ritualized tradition are also important, so that all classical Japanese gardens share the same visual "language."

This garden may be divided roughly into five sections, each following a different Japanese style. There is a shrine garden, a tea garden, and a dry landscape, or Zen garden. A hill garden makes a pleasant backdrop, while a central lawn area represents a Japanese "flat" garden.

Garden components
The most dramatic feature is the scaled-down dry landscape, or Zen garden, which is near the miniature teahouse and is accessed through a bamboo gate.

▶ **Stone lanterns** Originally used in shrines and temples for holding votive offerings, lanterns of various shapes and sizes light up meandering stepping-stone paths. Tradition dictates that the plants be of Japanese origin.

The dry stream is a distinctive Japanese feature. Pebbles fill an artificial channel, arranged to simulate the flow of water. Fine gravel or marble chips can also be used, and tiny pieces of slate, embedded in sand in mosaic patterns, will create the impression of moving water.

Stepping stones in the "flat garden" are laid in curving irregular lines, in keeping with Japanese tradition. Occasional large rocks are set among the smaller ones, as reminders of stone's endurance in a changing world. Some stepping stones are decorated with graphic symbols — four depict the seasons of the year.

Japanese rock gardens are far removed from Western-style ones. The rocks are the most important element and are chosen with care for their shape, color, and texture. There are strict rules for the correct grouping of the stones, which often represent particular concepts.

Stone lanterns of varied geometric shapes offer contrast to the more natural forms of plants and rocks. Lit at night, they illuminate the pathways and throw reflections in the water.

Woven bamboo panels, 6 ft (1.8 m) high, are attached to the boundary fencing and provide additional shelter. A dry landscape, or Zen garden, and miniature teahouse are concealed behind mature trees and shrubs.

The "well" is operated by concealed pipes. Water drips continually from a bucket suspended above a stone sink and splashes softly into the basin below. Water is symbolic of life and associated with purification.

The rocks set in the gravel may represent mountains, according to tradition, or islands in the sea, depending on their shape.

Teahouses are classed according to the number of floor mats they contain. This one, built of square-mesh wooden trellising, is a "four-and-a-half mat" teahouse.

The garden has three pools, the longest of which features a waterfall. In Japanese gardening water is an essential element, sometimes represented only symbolically, as in Zen gardens, but more often as actual streams and pools. Always referred to as a lake or sea, the pool — however small — is irregular in shape, and a stream should wind along naturally, perhaps splashing over a waterfall. The banks may be shored up with rocks or low-growing plants, or they may merge into a stretch of pebbly beach.

All the pools are serviced by circulating pumps, one operating a traditional "deer scarer." This is a bamboo pipe set on a pivot, which creates a regular, soft plonking sound. Another pump operates a water basin, where people can wash before partaking in the tea ceremony.

Three bridges can be found in the garden. One is a traditional stone half-moon bridge, another a simple stone slab with end stones on either side. The third consists of two stones, with a gap between, through which evil spirits will fall, according to folklore.

One striking stone feature is the result of a happy accident. An artificial stream, lined with flexible polyethylene covered with a layer of stones, sprang a leak just before the date of a garden tour, when hundreds of visitors were expected. As there was no time for repairs, the stones were temporarily rearranged to represent the tumbling flow of water. This

▼**Japanese garden design** The object of a true Japanese garden is to create a space of peace and quiet in which to contemplate nature and restore inner harmony.

THE ZEN GARDEN

▲ The entrance is through a bamboo gate, partly concealed by shrubs.

▶ The purest and highest form of Japanese gardening is the dry landscape, or Zen garden. This type of garden is not for active use; it is a place of contemplation that demands a response to the beauty of abstract shapes. In most Zen gardens, rocks are arranged as mountains in a symbolic sea of fine gravel, which is raked into different patterns every day, following strict tradition.

feature proved popular and has been allowed to remain.

In keeping with the Japanese tradition, the stepping-stones in the "flat garden" are not laid in straight lines, and occasional large stones are set among the smaller ones so that visitors can stop to rest or view the garden.

Some of the stepping-stones have graphic symbols: for example, four represent the seasons of the year. The stone symbolizing spring is the farthest from the house, as spring is traditionally the most longed-for season.

Stone lanterns cast candlelight on the pathways at night. The lanterns' more formal geometric shapes also offer contrast to the natural forms of plants and rocks.

A recent feature is a "well" made from a waterproofed old stone laundry sink placed slightly above ground level. On top of this is a woven bamboo lid, with a bucket suspended above. Concealed pipes and a circulating

pump help to create the illusion that the bucket has just been drawn from the well — water drips continually from the brim of the bucket onto the bamboo lid and into the basin below, making a pleasant soft sound.

Planting

Japanese plants usually thrive in the temperate parts of the United States, provided the soil and exposure are suitable.

Bamboos, rhododendrons, Japanese maples, Japanese ferns, conifers, and water plants make up the basic planting structure of this garden. Among the maples are *Acer palmatum* 'Dissectum Atropurpureum,' with deep purple leaves; *A. japonicum* 'Aureum,' with soft yellow leaves; and *A. palmatum* 'Osakazuki,' with green leaves that turn fiery scarlet in fall.

The bamboos include *Pleioblastus variegata*, which forms low, dense thickets of pale green

canes; *Thamnocalamus spathaceus*, an elegant species with bright green canes, maturing to a dull yellow-green; and *Pleioblastus auricoma*, a variegated bamboo with purplish-green canes and narrow dark green leaves, heavily striped with yellow.

The only Western plant in the garden is the corkscrew hazel (*Corylus avellana* 'Contorta'). This European shrub is, however, quite Oriental in appearance.

Flower power

Although many of the showiest flowering cherries, azaleas, rhododendrons, and camellias have Oriental origins, flowers play a secondary role in traditional Japanese gardens: form and foliage are all-important.

Flowering plants are part of this garden, however. They include Japanese clematises, Japanese rhododendrons, Japanese roses, and fall-blooming Japanese camellias. Most dramatic of all

▲ **Stone basin** An essential part of the ancient tea ceremony, a hollowed-out stone stands by the entrance to the teahouse. A bamboo water dipper rests on it, as tradition dictates.

are the Japanese wisterias, with their 3 ft (90 cm) long flower racemes; the lilac-flowered, fragrant *Wisteria floribunda* 'Macrobotrys'; and a white-flowered cultivar ('Alba').

Seasonal impact

For late-fall, winter, and early-spring interest, well over half the plants are evergreen. From midspring onward, the fresh colors of unfurling young deciduous leaves are a major feature, together with cherry blossoms and the orange-red blooms of the deciduous *Rhododendron japonicum*.

The Japanese maples turn brilliant yellow, orange, bronze, or red in fall — partnered by the bright orange seedpods of Chinese lanterns *(Physalis alkekengi)*.

An early-winter-flowering camellia, a cultivar of the species *Camellia sasanqua*, bears small, scented pink-flushed white flowers as well as gray-green leaves with white margins.

One unusual seasonal feature is a container that holds the traditional "plant of the month." In October, for example, a chrysanthemum takes pride of place; in January, a dwarf Japanese white pine *(Pinus parviflora)*; and in February, a flowering plum.

Maintenance

The garden has specific requirements for maintenance. Nearly all the plants in the garden are either shrubs, trees, or perennials, so there is no need for transplanting or bedding out. A small

▲ **Dragon-eye pine** A young *Pinus densiflora* 'Oculus-draconis' unites the enduring elements of water and stone. In the foreground is a Japanese cedar *(Cryptomeria japonica)*.

▼ **Half-moon bridge** Spanning a dry-stream bed, a traditional stone bridge is almost concealed by a clump of variegated bamboos and the colorful foliage of Japanese maples.

▲ **Stone Buddha** Close to the statue is a container that holds the "plant of the month." This partnership represents the unchanging and the transient.

▼ **Traditional elements** Trees (especially conifers), shrubs, and ground cover are more important than transient flowers in a Japanese garden.

greenhouse provides all the winter shelter needed (in this climate) for the hardy bonsai trees.

In Japanese terms, the garden is overplanted, so a fair amount of pruning and thinning is needed. Bamboos are cut back hard in winter. To keep the plants small, they receive no fertilizer at all.

The main pool is covered with a net in fall to keep out leaves and protect the valuable koi carp from marauding cats. To prevent the pool from icing over completely in winter, logs are floated in it. The gaps that remain between the logs and the surrounding ice allow enough oxygen into the water to support the carp, who sink to the pool's deepest point.

Stepping-stones are always watered before guests arrive, as Japanese gardens are traditionally supposed to look their freshest immediately after a rain.

Grass lawns are not often a part of Oriental gardens — moss is more commonly used. In time the central grass area will be replaced with a moss surface. Mosslike pearlwort *(Sagina subulata)* was tried here but looked too golden, so mosses will be used instead. They thrive and spread in light shade and moist soil. Raked sand, a mulch of fine gravel or pine needles, or tamped earth are other traditional alternatives to grass.

Japanese ornaments

Statuary and stone ornaments are of less importance in Japanese gardens than in Western ones. Originally, they were purely functional or had religious significance; even today they are used with restraint.

Stone lanterns have been used for centuries, not for decoration, but to light a bend in a path, a bridge over a stream, or the entrance to the teahouse. Traditionally, a candlelit lantern is placed so that it is half-hidden by overhanging branches or shrouded by foliage plants at its base.

Stone basins also belong to the ancient past. Carved from natural stone, they may be round or square, smooth or elaborately carved. Traditionally, they were near the teahouse so that arriving guests could wash their hands.

ACKNOWLEDGMENTS

Photo credits
Peter Baistow 161-166; Karen Bussolini 36, 39 (t), 112; Eric Crichton 9(b), 10(t,c), 12, 21(t), 22, 43(b), 79-84, 131(t), (designer Peter Aldington) 155-160, (designer Graham Bell) 103-108, (designers Chris and Freda Norton) 91-96; Eaglemoss/Eric Crichton 45-50, 111, 114-116, 123-128, (designer Wendy Wright) 97-102; Eaglemoss/Andrew Lawson (designers Mr. and Mrs. Kenneth Watson) 167-172; ECC Quarries Ltd 10(b); Garden Picture Library (John Glover) 78, (Marijke Heuff) 143-149, (Ron Sutherland) 38(t), 61-63, 110, 149-154, (Brigitte Thomas) 2-3, (Steven Wooster) 130-131; John Glover front cover; Jerry Harpur (designer Michael Blood) 55-60, (designer Geoff Kaye) 137-142, (designer Arthur Turner) 29-34; Neil Holmes 9(t), 38(b),(designer Colin Wells-Brown) 65-70; Insight Photo Library (Linda Burgess) 131(b),

(Michelle Garrett) 129; Georges Leveque (designer Erwan Tynan) 85-90; S and O Mathews 39(b), 42-43; Tania Midgley 23, 42(b), 43(t), 133(b), 134; Monarch Aluminium Ltd 11(t); John Neubauer 51-54, 64; Clive Nichols 4-5, 8, 11(b), 14; Hugh Palmer 21(b), 28; Philippe Perdereau/Brigitte Thomas 37, 40, (designer Lesne) 71-76; Photos Horticultural 132; Harry Smith Collection 117-122, 133(t); Elizabeth Whiting and Associates (Michael Nicholson) 6, 136; Rita Wuethrian 13.

Illustrators
Lynn Chadwick 66, 81, 86-87, 104-105, 118-119, 146-147, 156-157, 162-163; Russell Gordon-Smith 25, 26; Dee McLean 27; Vivien Monument 19, 24, 72-73, 98-99, 139; Lindy Norton 20, 22, 23; Coral Mula 15-16; Liz Pepperell 17-18, 47, 50, 56, 113, 127.

Index compiled by Sydney Wolfe Cohen

Reader's Digest Production

Assistant Production Supervisor: Mike Gallo
Electronic Prepress Support: Karen Goldsmith
Quality Control Manager: Ann Kennedy Harris
Assistant Production Manager: Dexter Street

Book Production Director: Ken Gillett
Prepress Manager: Garry Hansen
Book Production Manager: Joe Leeker
U.S. Prepress Manager: Mark P. Merritt